ERWIN BAUER'S BEAR IN THEIR WORLD

ERWIN BAUER'S
BEAR
IN THEIR WORLD

By Erwin A. Bauer
Photos by Erwin A. and Peggy Bauer

Published by Outdoor Life Books
New York

Published by
  Popular Science Books
  Sedgewood® Press
  750 Third Avenue
  New York, New York 10017

Distributed by Meredith Corporation, Des Moines, Iowa.

Produced by Soderstrom Publishing Group Inc.
Book design by J.C. Suarès
Design/production by Laurence Ian Burns

Library of Congress Cataloging-in-Publication Data
Bauer, Erwin A.
   Erwin Bauer's Bear in their world.
   Bibliography: p.
   Includes index.
   1. Bears. 2. Mammals—North America. I. Title.
II. Title: Bear in their world.
QL737.C27B38 1985   599.74′446   85–18779
ISBN 0-696-11094-6

Manufactured in the United States of America

10 9 8 7 6 5 4 3 2

CONTENTS

PREFACE

Early in the 18th century, a British officer serving in the American colonies went on a black-bear hunt with Ojibwa Indians. He wrote in a letter home how astounded he was to see one Indian stroke a bear the Indian had killed, kiss it and call it Grandmother, beg its forgiveness, and then whisper into its ear that "the Englishman" had shot it. The guilt that Indian apparently felt more than 200 years ago may be exactly what many of us feel today.

During the months I spent writing this book—and the many years I've photographed the outdoors—I became increasingly aware of our carelessness toward the land ever since the Pilgrims arrived. The ongoing elimination of bears is sad testimony to that carelessness.

The first wild bears I ever saw were those of Yellowstone National Park when in 1935, at age 16, I hitchhiked from Ohio to work there. My job was dressing trout and swabbing out dirty fishing boats at the rental dock, then near Fishing Bridge. I will never forget that glorious summer. I could catch more fish in a few hours after work than in a month at home. That year, in the depth of the Great Depression, there were almost as many black bears roaming around Fishing Bridge as there were human travelers. I cannot recall having any trouble with those bears, or even with the occasional grizzly. Instead, the bears stimulated my lifelong fascination with them.

Aldo Leopold, conservationist and father of America's system of wilderness areas, once commented that the more familiar you become with bears, the more you admire and even love them, or the more you hate them, depending on your viewpoint. My wife Peggy and I have long watched bears, photographed them, and sometimes practically lived with them. We have studied and admired bears for long hours through viewfinders and telephoto lenses. These hours have been tremendously exciting and rewarding.

The last bears Peggy and I saw before I sat down to write this book were the magnificent grizzlies of Denali National Park, Alaska. We spent an entire August there, observing and filming grizzlies from Sable Pass and the Toklat River flats to Thorofare Pass and Wonder Lake. We probably saw 20 different bears during that period, several of them many times. We learned to identify some by their color, size, unusual markings, and even their unique behavior. Several became old "friends." Despite the often gloomy weather, that summer was as glorious for me as my first summer in Yellowstone so many years before.

Bears have received negative publicity in recent years because of an unusual number of bear-man incidents, including the deaths of tourists. As a result, there has been new pressure to get rid of bears—particularly in national parks—at a time when concerned scientists and conservationists are trying to save the few remaining grizzlies at Yellowstone. Time will tell which side wins out.

This much, however, is certain: What remains of the American wilderness would be a much poorer place without bears. Tramping on a Rocky Mountain trail would not provide the same zest, the same sense of expectation, if bears did not live there in the wild. No other native creatures have ever excited our imagination and our spirit of adventure as much. Bears belong in outdoor North America—living free.

This book is about the many bears we have met. It is also about their life histories, compiled by dedicated biologists, many of whom are our friends. Here I also write on the history, lore, and mystique of bears so that every reader may understand them better.

My work on this book was a labor of love, even though man's threat to bears has often made this work bittersweet.

Erwin A. Bauer
Teton Village, Wyoming

CHAPTER 1
BLACK BEARS

I spent an unforgettable April of 1957 near DeTour, Michigan, on a fishing-story assignment for *Outdoor Life* magazine. The winter had been hard and bitter. With the onset of warm weather, bears were appearing all over. Everyone on the Upper Peninsula had his own bear story, some of which might sound comical today.

The "bear season" had begun officially when a pulpwood cutter near Rudyard heard a commotion nearby, turned, and found a bruin watching him, clutching his metal lunch box about 25 feet away. Next thing the forester knew he was in the crown of a tree looking down at the bear. It was the first time in his life, he told me, he had ever been so high above ground without a stepladder. The bear calmly pried open the lunch box and ate the forester's fried chicken and potato salad. Then it wandered away.

Black bears in spring might be ornery or inquisitive, hungry or disoriented, or just groggy following their long winter hibernation. That same day at Whitefish Point, construction workers found a bruin snoozing comfortably in the cab of a crane. They tried to chase the bear away from the machinery, but it only circled, hesitated, and climbed back into an open door of the cab. One workman quickly slammed the door, figuring he would lock the bear safely inside until a game warden could come and remove it. He did not realize that the crane operator was also in the cab. Wisely, the operator did

Omnivorous, the black bear will even search for insects under the bark of a fallen birch.

not argue with the bear; he dove out the opposite window and only dislocated one shoulder.

On Sugar Island a presumably hungry bear tried to enter a cottage where the smell of cooking meat was strong. The occupant, a former professional wrestler, tried to slam the door shut on the bear, but was only partially successful. The match ended in a draw, with the wrestler holding the door part way shut against the bear's neck until a neighbor's hound dogs arrived and began to bite the bear's behind. They drove the bear out of the vicinity.

Two days later a night watchman on Drummond Island came home after midnight to find that a bear had broken into his kitchen pantry and eaten a large pastie (a local meat pie) set out for him as a snack. The wet, late winter weather had warped the pantry door so that the lock wouldn't catch, thus letting the bear push it in.

After that the watchman's distraught wife slept with a loaded rifle beside her. This made each night's homecoming a sort of Russian roulette for the husband, who never knew what kind of welcome he would receive. Finally he stayed home from work long enough to shoot the bear when it returned, presumably for more pasties.

Still more transpired near DeTour this remarkable Michigan springtime. Watching from her window at dusk one evening, a housewife saw two men approaching the house. In the dim light she recognized her husband by his gait, but couldn't make out his companion. Being hospitable, she went to the door and called out, "Who's your friend, Fred?"

"Friend?" her husband replied. He turned around and nearly jumped out of his boots. He hit the ground running headlong toward the yellow light in his front door. His "friend" had been a large bear, apparently just ambling along quietly behind him and sniffing the load of groceries he carried. That bruin turned, vanished into the darkness, and was never seen there again.

Spring is when black bears are usually most visible and most likely to be encountered. Despite their notoriety, black bears are rarely seen by humans in the wild. Rather, they are most common in zoos and on television, where Smokey, the Forest Service bear, became an institution. Not even the most dedicated enthusiasts of local bear country are certain to ever meet Smokey's real-life counterpart—at least, not very often. The black bear is simply a shy, retiring, and elusive animal. Nonetheless, black bears have always had significant impact on life and legend in North America.

BLACK BEARS AND
THE AMERICAN FRONTIER

From the day the first Europeans waded ashore on the eastern seaboard, men and black bears have been antagonists. Only in recent decades have we developed a fresh new philosophy of stewardship. Many of us now feel much more kindly toward bears, and we want to be certain that they survive on earth as long as we do.

Killing a bear was considered an act of bravery among many of the American Indians. Bear teeth and claws were badges of courage, like military campaign ribbons. Early white settlers felt the same way. Between wars and Indian skirmishes, a young man could best prove himself by killing a bruin, especially a troublesome one. Young Daniel Boone was thus moved to carve his now well-known "D. Boone killed a bar by this tree" on a Kentucky sycamore. Something akin to hero worship was the reward for the champion bear-slayer in any frontier community. Bears were the enemy. This attitude often led to bizarre incidents, such as this one related by Ohio author George Laycock.

About 1799, a George Cochran migrated to the Ohio frontier from Virginia and homesteaded where the Scioto River empties into the Ohio River. One day he spotted a black bear swimming in the Scioto. Although his gun was in his cabin some distance away, Cochran did not hesitate to push off in his canoe into the murky current in hot pursuit. His strategy was as simple as it was ill-conceived. He planned to keep prodding the bear into deep water until it drowned, when he would recover its dead body. Cochran was apparently unaware of the great tenacity of a healthy adult black bear.

The bear, realizing its predicament, turned and swam directly toward its pursuer. As the angry animal climbed into the bow of the canoe, Cochran jumped out of the stern. He then stood chest-deep in the Scioto, sadly watching his valuable craft with a bear aboard disappear downstream. Indeed, all black bears soon vanished from the broad Scioto Valley, which today is a mixture of bottomland cornfields and smoky industrial development.

Perhaps because of their nature and reclusiveness, black bears have fared better on this continent than have other bears or many other large animals. Black bears are probably much more intelligent than most other mammals, according to tests of the Psychology Department at the University of Tennessee. Like all forest dwellers, they are difficult if not impossible to see, let alone count. Naturalist-writer Ernest Thompson Seton estimated the continental black-bear population at 2 million before the arrival of Columbus. Today's leading bear scientists set the total at about 200,000, or about one-tenth of Seton's figure. In the mid-1980s blacks survived in at least token numbers in 30 of the 49 states where the species originally occurred. Bears still exist in all Canadian provinces and territories, as well as in a few scattered parts of Mexico.

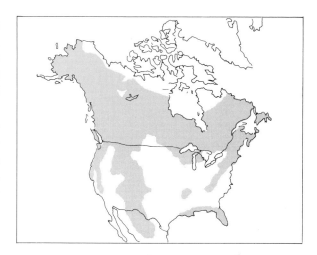

The range of the black bear is one of the most extensive of all large North American mammals.

Most black bears within the United States are found in the West, where large tracts of wilderness or semi-wilderness remain. Washington State has the largest bear population with an estimated 27,000 to 30,000. West Virginia and Kentucky still boast of bear populations, but Daniel Boone may have met as many in a week's wandering as

High meadows with aspens and conifers characterize this northern New Mexico bear country—a lonely wilderness where black bears do not encounter many people.

This adult male black bear was photographed on the edge of a northern Michigan forest. All around were large felled trees, with dense brush taking over—a cover black bears often seek in summer when it offers a variety of edible plants. The black "spots" in this photo are blackflies, tormenting the bear.

the few dozen that now cling to existence in both those states. As recently as 1945, the southeastern United States contained a fairly large, healthy population of black bears, estimated at 12,000 to 13,000. But biologists believe there are now fewer than 3,000 left, with about one-third of those in Virginia. Changing or vanishing habitat has been most responsible for this distressing decline. But both the proliferation of feral hogs, which compete with bears for food, and widespread poaching have had an impact, too, as has an ongoing market for bear's teeth, hides, claws and skulls.

RELATIVE SIZES

According to most popular accounts, there is virtually no such thing as a small bear. No hunter or irate farmer, it seems, has ever slain one that was not a snarling giant with yellow teeth exposed, about to tear the man apart. Yet the actual weights and dimensions of bears—either dead or alive—rarely justify the fantastic claims that reach the press every year.

The black is the smallest of North American bears. Though 600-pounders have been found, the species seldom exceeds a weight of 500 pounds, or a length of 5½ feet, if measured with the bear lying on its back from nose tip to

tail tip. A mature adult stands about 3 feet at the front shoulder.

Consider the following weight figures compiled over a number of years in Pennsylvania. Yearlings (12 months old) average 105 pounds; two-year-old bears average 155 pounds; three-year-olds average 205 pounds; four-year-olds average 255 pounds; and five-year-olds average 305 pounds. Males are one-fourth to one-fifth larger than females of the same age. And, the weight of any bruin can fluctuate greatly from spring through late fall.

According to Minnesota-based bear biologist Dr. Lynn Rogers, the growth rates among wild Pennsylvania bears are among the fastest in North America. Growth rates in northern Minnesota, with long severe winters, are about half that of Pennsylvania's, unless the bears eat a lot of garbage, in which case they can become as heavy as blacks anywhere. One September, Rogers sedated and weighed a garbage-fed black bear that tipped the scales at 611 pounds.

Ed Strobel shot a possible record 585-pounder, also dressed weight, in 1953 in Vilas County, Wisconsin. This could have tipped the scales close to 700 pounds when alive.

It would be a mistake to claim that any one of the numerous reports of giant black bears describes the largest ever. The older the claim, the more likely it is to have expanded with time. But it is worth noting that in 1885, what was described as the granddaddy of all black bears was shot in Wisconsin. It weighed 802½ pounds on "honest scales," according to somewhat official reports.

Another of the largest documented black bears weighed alive (and later released) was a 605-pounder captured at a garbage dump near Tupper Lake in New York's Adirondacks. The bear was extremely fat from its unnatural garbage diet, and state conservation researchers estimated its age at somewhere between five and ten years. In 1955, a hunter shot a male in Essex County that weighed 562 pounds dressed weight. Alive, it would have been 95 pounds heavier than the Tupper Lake bear.

An exceptionally big, well-fed black before hibernation may tip the scales at slightly over 600 pounds.

Now let's look at perhaps the most important statistic of all. Assume you are hiking in bear country. You see a black bear. Chances are it will be coal black in color, and weigh 220 to 230 pounds. That is the average weight nationwide for this species, according to weight statistics from 15 states.

Bears in the northern part of their range will likely be on the heavy end of this average at 230 pounds. In the South they will likely weigh a little less.

But weight is not the only way to measure and compare the size or even the health of one bear with another. The Boone and Crockett Club, custodian of big-game trophy records, uses a system whereby one measures the length and width of the skull, then adds the two dimensions together for a final score. Of course a bear has to be dead, skinned, and fleshed to become a statistic this way. Although black bears with the largest skull measurements also tend to be heavier bears, and vice versa, there is no absolute correlation between the two. But by Boone and Crockett reckoning, the all-time record black bear had a skull measurement of $23^{10}/_{16}$ inches and was found in Utah. In fact the top ten largest skulls came from the West.

PHYSIQUE AND PHYSIOLOGY

Black bears share their range with grizzlies in parts of the northern Rockies, western Canada, and Alaska. Because a black can be brown to cinnamon in color and nearly as large as many grizzlies (although usually much smaller on av-

Record skull sizes for black bears approach 15 inches in length and 9 inches in width.

erage), distinguishing between the two may not be easy. That task becomes even harder in poor illumination, or deep in a forest, or when the animal is moving and far away. The excitement factor can also make an inexperienced person mistake one for the other, and many of the "grizzlies" sighted are really large old black bears.

Viewed from the side, a black bear does not have the noticeable front shoulder hump of the grizzly. Blacks have longer, thinner snouts than grizzlies, which have wider, more concave faces. A grizzly also has a more swaggering, swinging, pigeon-toed gait that an experienced person can recognize almost immediately.

If you see any North American bear in a tree, or climbing one, it is almost surely a black bear. Small grizzlies have been seen climbing, though their long and relatively straight claws make this a slow, difficult process. The black bear's shorter, curved claws grip most kinds of tree bark well enough so that the animal can practically run up a tree. Cubs are able to climb soon after leaving the dens where they are born. Black bears have been seen in trees, feeding on fruits and nuts, and even sleeping on large limbs, feet hanging down. Unless the tree is very short, a black bear descends rear-end first, sliding and clutching at the trunk with its claws.

Two kinds of hair cover the bodies of black bears. The soft, dense underfur functions mainly as insulation against intense cold. The guard hair, longer and much thicker in diameter than the underfur, also insulates against the cold, and serves yet another purpose. The guard hair helps conceal the bear from prey or enemies, and may even convey behavioral information in the same way most other animals use odors (or pheromones) to communicate fear, aggression, or sexual readiness to members of the same species.

Annual shedding of both guard hair and underfur begins in late spring—usually May or earlier in the Southeast, and June in the North. Shedding is gradual, though a black bear may temporarily appear shaggy as it begins growing new coat (starting with new guard hairs) while shedding the old. But by late August in the North and by mid-autumn elsewhere, the underfur becomes noticeably thicker. Toward the end of fall, the black bear's pelage is heavy and protective enough

This Minnesota black bear had no trouble climbing this tree, though the bear weighed 250 pounds or more. If pursued by hounds, a black bear can claw its way up a tall tree at a full run.

for the bear to survive any winter, either above or beneath the ground.

Except for the claws, the hind footprint of an average adult black is shaped similarly to a human footprint, and measures about 7 or 8 inches long by 4 inches wide. But most of the time, the heel of the hind foot does not show unless the bear is walking in soft mud or deep snow. The fore footprint averages about 4 inches by 4 inches. When a black bear is running, the hind footprints will appear just in front of those of the forefeet. When walking, the hind footprints usually appear in the fore footprints.

A final interesting dimension of black bears is dental. The canine teeth of an adult are from 2 to over 3 inches apart, and long enough to each inflict a nasty wound about ½-inch in diameter. That's inducement enough to stay clear of a black bear's jaws at all costs.

COLORATION

Seven or eight of every ten black bears nationwide are black, usually with a small white or cream throat patch. The farther east a bruin lives in the United States or Canada, the more likely it is to be pure black. Yet no other American mammal exists in so many color phases. Next to black, the most common color of the pelage is a rich chocolate brown. The pelage also comes in all shades of brown, including cinnamon, tan, and even straw. Each cub in a single litter (two or three at most) may be a different color, although they tend to be either all black or all brown. Many years ago in Yellowstone Park, I saw a dark-brown roadside sow with triplets that were black, brown, and cinnamon. The foursome spent an entire summer freeloading from passing tourists near West Thumb.

There are two striking subspecies of black, both very restricted in range and both living toward the northern limits of the black-bear belt. I have been lucky enough to see both of them. One, the Kermode bear of British Columbia, was an off-white to cream color. Today it roams ghost-

Pages 22 through 24: These profiles of an adult black bear perfectly illustrate the distinctive profile of the species. The black does not have the grizzly's shoulder hump or heavy muzzle.

The short curved claws of the black bear are ideally suited for the climbing of trees.

like only on one cool, often misty coastal island where it is totally protected. It is not an albino but rather a true subspecies that generally breeds true to its pale color, although not always. The other unique black bear is the blue, or glacier, subspecies, which I watched briefly long ago near Glacier Bay, Alaska. From a distance it seemed to be a slate gray in color, but others have described it as bluish-silvery-gray, blue woodsmoke, or iron-colored. This blue bear lives in an awesomely beautiful mountain land punctuated with glaciers that "flow" all the way to the edge of the Pacific Ocean. Though all black bears live in beautiful places, this elusive blue subspecies may live in the most splendid of all.

Many black bears tend to become grizzled around the muzzle and flanks in extreme old age. It is most noticeable on the solid black individuals. In strong backlight or sidelight, this grizzling can make a black bear resemble a grizzly. Also, some of the very light, tan-colored black bears become darker as they reach maturity.

Why are black bears more likely to be black in eastern North America than in the West? A likely explanation is Gloger's Rule: Among warm-blooded creatures, black pigments are most prevalent in warm humid areas, while reds and yellows are more prevalent in drier areas, as in the West. Since brown-phase black bears can better tolerate the sun's heat, they can feed a little longer

every day in open areas. They can therefore gain weight faster than black colored bears, produce cubs at an earlier age, and have larger litters. Thus, in the drier, more open, environment of the West, the brown bear's tolerance to heat gives it a selective advantage over black ones.

Black bears are essentially solitary animals. Except for family groups—and except around certain garbage dumps, which act as magnets for any kind of bruins—I have never seen two or more adult black bears together. Obviously males and females must meet and mingle during the short breeding season, which runs from May to August, depending on the latitude. But this breeding must be private indeed, because the available scientific literature on black bears contains little on the subject.

BEARS INVADING CIVILIZED AREAS

As a result of failed wild berry and nut crops, bears sometimes begin turning up in and around certain communities looking for food. People sometimes mistake this phenomenon for a bear population explosion. In the early 1980s Fairbanks, Alaska, had bears materializing everywhere. In summer, 1970, black bears seemed to swarm around Lake Nipissing, Ontario. A typical bear invasion took place in the summer of 1949 in northeastern Minnesota, following a year when bear complaints were almost nonexistent. The trouble started when bears invaded campsites in the Ely and Grand Marais vicinities, both popular with summertime tourists. Tents were torn up, food supplies were sacked, and canoes were damaged—due probably to the lingering odor of fish. These same bears fought with one another at garbage dumps and managed to enter even the sturdiest vacation homes, referred to almost universally by natives as "cabins." Damage was high from Duluth all the way to the Canadian border. In fact, the police forces of Duluth and Two Harbors were receiving five calls an hour about bear disturbances during the month of August.

At least two bears walked into the small tourist town of Ely. One, which strolled into a sporting goods shop, had to be shot. The game warden of Two Harbors reported 38 bears definitely terminated in his immediate area, though he believed the actual number to be about 75. One bruin broke into a hog farm, and another into a large chicken coop through a ventilator that was smashed in the process. After dining on pork-chops and fryers, the two left a trail of white feathers in their wake for a long distance.

In desperation, the local game warden set up three feeding areas around Duluth. The idea was to attract the bears away from town to easier pickings. It worked, though all too well in one instance. A feeding station near a gas station on Highway 53 attracted so many quarreling bears and so many inquisitive humans that a severe traffic problem developed. *Life* magazine carried a story on this fiasco, as well as one on a bruin swimming in nearby Lake Superior that climbed into a boat already occupied by three anglers. The men were forced to bail out, one of them minus a piece of his trousers. The last thing they saw was a bruin enjoying a boat ride on the great-est Great Lake.

What caused the bear invasion of 1949 in northeastern Minnesota? According to an official report, wild food supplies were scarce that year. So were acorns, and all the normally abundant berry crops had apparently failed. Plus, a large population of cubs that had survived the previous two years. By mid-September of that year, nui-sance complaints came to a end and the invasion was over.

FOOD-RELATED BEHAVIOR

The scarcity or abundance of natural food has much to do with black-bear behavior. It may ex-plain why in 1956, near Saranac Lake, New York, a 300-pound male was feeding on the freshly killed carcass of a half-grown cub. The canni-balistic bruin had eaten all but the head and fore-quarters of the cub, which might have weighed 50 or 60 pounds alive. Cannibalism is far from unknown among American bears, and females have been observed both driving bears away from their cubs and leading cubs in a wide detour around nearby males.

Dr. Lynn Rogers has often found starvation among young, northeastern Minnesota black bears when the berry and nut crops have failed. There's also record of an old male in Maine that had tried

to capture a porcupine. Its muzzle was so infested with quills that it could not longer eat. When found by lumberjacks, it was all but ready for recycling.

A black bear will eat almost anything biode-gradable, and a few things that aren't. It will explore and wander for miles in search of calories as if it had a built-in contour map of the land. The bear will then gorge itself until its stomach can hold no more, sleep it off, and start the pro-cess all over again. The physical makeup of the species, especially its dental structure, classifies it as a carnivore. But in practice, bears are om-nivorous. Their food ranges from nuts, berries, fruits, grasses, and forbs, to livestock and any kind of carrion.

In some regions bears eat enormous quantities of worms, grubs, ants, and insects of any kind. They have been known to catch fish in shallow streams, to dig up hibernating rodents and fox cubs from their dens, to pillage mouse nests (eat-ing nest and all), and to rob bird nests.

In Okefenokee Swamp, Georgia, a fishing guide told me he saw a black bear invade an egret rookery during the spring nesting period. The bear ate the young birds, which were still unable to fly, in the nests it could easily reach. But when it tried to reach a nest high in a dead tree, the tree toppled under the bear's weight. The bruin came crashing to the ground underneath the trunk, quickly recovered, and pounced on three fallen egret chicks.

Black bears never wander aimlessly. They are

Wild grapes are among the countless fruits, growing all over America, on which a black bear thrives and grows fat for winter.

Black bears exist in every color from cream to coal black (the most common by far), though brown-phase blacks are not unusual in the western United States.

Almost all eastern black bears are black. They commonly have a light-colored throat patch. Color phases become increasingly common in the West.

The reddish, or cinnamon-colored, bear may be the black bear's most handsome color phase. This one was photographed in summer in Washington.

On Kermode Island, British Columbia, a race of cream-colored "ghost" bears stalks the evergreen forests. These are the lightest of all black-bear color phases, and normally breed true to type.

Black bears remained fairly numerous throughout the southeastern United States until the beginning of the 20th century, when an abrupt decline began. Today in the South they survive almost entirely in large swamp areas in the Great Smoky and other mountain lands.

always seeking better, more plentiful sources of food, sex, (during breeding season), or both. If not for the fact that most black bears can be attracted—or baited—fairly easily to human food, they would rarely be shot. From the time it is a year or so old, a black bear is already more shy and elusive than any adult whitetail buck. The bear's scenting ability, eyesight, and hearing are all superior to the deer's. But food is something it cannot resist; bears are not picky eaters.

APPETITE FOR TROUBLE

Farmers are among those who least appreciate a bear's huge appetite. Bears enter barnyards and corrals to kill calves, sheep, and pigs with swift blows from their paws, rather than by hugging, as is commonly believed. Small animals are often dispatched with a bite at the base of the neck. Keep in mind that most bears seldom raid livestock or chicken coops. But when a bear learns to do this through hunger, parental example, or by accident, it is probably hooked forever. The bear will almost certainly keep coming back until it is shot. And just one culprit bear in a community gives all a bad name.

A study of black-bear predation in Maine revealed sheep to be by far the most frequently attacked livestock. The reason may be the sheep's stupidity and reaction to danger. In most cases, the bear would drag the carcass away to a concealed location and devour it at leisure. Often the udder, brisket, and stomach were the first parts eaten.

Many farmers and ranchers have charged that black bears kill for the sake of killing because, sometimes, little or nothing is eaten. That may be true in isolated cases, but there is another explanation for this phenomenon. In the midst of a milling flock of terrified sheep, the bear may itself become confused and start striking out on all sides with its powerful forepaws. Any sheep nearby are then killed or injured, while the bear may then be frightened away without carrying off a kill.

The Maine study reached some other conclusions. Most bear attacks on sheep occurred in pastures well removed from occupied buildings, or where there were no people from spring through

In this photo a young black bear is testing the air with its extremely sensitive nose to detect any promise of food or sign of danger. The black bear's scenting ability is superior to that of any other large mammals.

fall—grazing season in the North. Pastures adjacent to woods, where bears had a concealed approach to the prey were also poor herding areas. The presence of dogs, however, tended to intimidate bears.

Bears can develop a fondness for oats, green corn, and garden vegetables. I once inspected the aftermath of a bear's nighttime foray into a northern Wisconsin cornfield. After eating most of the ears in a half acre or so, the bear rolled and wallowed in the field, flattening row after row of cornstalks to the ground. On other occasions, the landowner told me, this or another bear had been satisfied just to tear off the ears of corn and carry them away into the adjacent woods. He also noted that the green corn diet appeared to give the thief a bad case of loose bowels.

If vegetables and unguarded sheep are tempting to a roving bear, beehives, honey, and the plump young larvae of bees can be irresistible. Many a bruin has suffered terrible stinging all over its face and around its eyes, ears, and lips just to rob a hive—wild or domestic.

In the dry June of 1963, the Batchewana fire tower near Sault-Sainte Marie, Ontario, reported blue smoke and blaze in nearby timber. Fire rangers soon found a blazing fire in the dense under-

This black bear has climbed onto the toppled birch trunk to scratch for insects in the rotting wood. It also probed with its long tongue just under the peeling birchbark.

brush. In the ashes they found the charred body of a 200-pound black bear. It was the victim of its own curiosity and sweet tooth.

The inquisitive bear apparently mistook the humming of a low-hanging Great Lakes power line for a busy beehive. Standing on its hind legs on a high bank, it managed to grab the power line with a forepaw. It was instantly electrocuted, and the flash sparked the brushfire. A year later, another black bear in nearby Michigan climbed a tall power pole to investigate the bee-like buzzing on top. This bear was also electrocuted.

The greatest bear-beehive problems occur in the Southeast, especially in Florida, where the best remaining bear country is also high-quality bee range. Woodlands of this type are normally too wet to produce pine for pulp or other timber. But they are lush with swamp and hammock plants such as palmetto, cabbage palm, sparkleberry,

◄ *Northern black bears may be found grazing in and around the edges of swamps, especially early in the summer. There are scattered reports of bruins wallowing on very hot days—possibly as a respite from biting insects.*

huckleberry, gallberry, holly, gum, yaupon, titi, locust, laurel, and haw. These plants are favored by bears, and also produce a rich and tasty flow of honey. Some bears develop an uncanny ability to find beekeepers' hives. No wonder Florida beekeepers hate all bears or even the thought of them.

Electric fences, numerous chemical repellents, booby traps, and noisemakers have been useless against determined beehive-robbing bears. So some beekeepers turned to poisons and set-guns, both of which were dangerous to other creatures as well as to humans. During the early 1950s, beekeepers killed approximately 175 bears a year, which was more than the annual legal kill by hunters. That toll, and a shrinking wilderness, threatened the black bear's survival in Florida.

As a result, conservation agencies and the University of Florida cooperated in a serious effort to keep bears away from woodland and swamp apiaries. Eventually, cantilevered, elevated platforms proved the most successful deterrents. Not only did these structures keep hives well above seasonal floodwaters, their overhangs prevented even the most agile and clever bear from clawing

These bears are feeding on a horse that had to be shot after a trail accident. Black bears can detect the odor of carrion from miles away.

This bear is most likely marking a territory with claw scratches on a tree trunk.

its way to the top. But bears still try to reach the sweet, sticky hoard they can smell; there are few of these platforms in the Florida backcountry that do not have multiple claw-marks on their supporting posts.

A more recent example of black-bear mischief concerns two scientists who were studying the breeding of endangered eastern bluebirds at the Camp LeJeune Marine Base. Part of their work involved putting up artificial nesting boxes on fence posts to replace the loss of natural nesting sites. Over a two-year period, black bears clawed, chewed, and knocked down 45 boxes from their posts, and ate the eggs or nestlings inside. The scientists wondered if, after finding edibles in one bluebird box, the bear didn't begin searching specifically for other boxes as a regular source of food.

BEAR SIGN

Any keen observer who walks often or far through black-bear country will see much more bear sign than actual bears—if he sees any bears at all. Bear trees are the most visible signs. There

are two kinds of bear trees. One, striped with claw marks, is often found along well-traveled trails, and still has naturalists puzzled. It has been written, romantically, that bears use these as measuring posts to mark their growth and indicate their reach. More likely, bruins use these trees, as do dogs and foxes, as scent stations to mark territories and as communication posts. Such bear trees may be signposts to warn other bears to keep clear. One such tree, a lodgepole pine, grows beside a hiking trail not far from where I live. I can just reach the highest claw marks, about 8 feet above the ground.

The other kind of bear tree is easy to find in some northern forests today. Instead of just stripping the trunk, leaving it dripping with sap, the bears girdle some completely. This damage leaves the tree open to insect attack and disease. A forest ranger in the Snoqualmie National Forest once showed me where several acres of potential timber had been similarly multilated by bears. Although most of this type of damage occurs in the Northwest, bears have also stripped conifer stands in Maine for fresh sap and sapwood.

There is a good explanation for the bear-tree

dilemma. It originates with the modern logging practice called clear-cutting, which means cutting all of the trees in a given tract, rather than selectively harvesting only the largest and most mature trees. Lumber companies claim that clear-cutting is the most economical, practical way to harvest timber. From their standpoint, it is indeed the most profitable method. But whether clear-cutting should be tolerated as a long-range forestry practice on our public lands might well be debated.

LOGGING

Clear-cut logging is a tremendous ecological shock to all the plants and animals of the area. The climax (fully mature) plants are suddenly replaced with new growth—*if* the soil is not washed away immediately following the clear-cutting process, as often happens in steep places. Those new plants make good habitat for bears and for other wildlife. The bear population may even explode and prosper as it has in parts of Washington and Oregon, until second-growth trees begin to shade out the berries and other low-level plants. Under such conditions of less food for more bears, the animals resort to substitute foods of lower nutritional value. These substitute foods include the sapwood of young conifers, which may have been planted at considerable expense. To the timber industry, the black bear ranks with fungus, fire, and the gypsy moth as enemies to be annihilated.

The paradox is that clear-cutting has forced Smokey the Bear to damage the forests he was created to protect. During the 1960s and 1970s, a lot of black bears were eliminated on federal lands, though they were often eliminated almost entirely on commercial forest lands and tree farms. The sad truth is that modern forestry philosophy simply contains no niche for black bears. It's geared more toward plywood and fast profits.

BLACK BEARS AND SALMON

Black bears were blamed for diminishing salmon runs in British Columbia and Alaska, even though clear-cutting and other destructive lumbering practices were the culprits. I have seen many once-fine, clear salmon-spawning streams so choked with the mud and debris of such logging, especially on Admiralty Island, that the fish could not possibly spawn or even swim far enough upstream to find washed-gravel spawning beds. Although not well known, black bears also fish for salmon in some southeastern Alaska streams, and they have been blamed by commercial netters for declining salmon catches.

While a student at the University of Alaska in the 1970s, biologist George Frame spent a summer studying the behavior of black bears and their impact on the salmon run of Olsen Creek, Prince William Sound, about 130 miles east of Anchorage. Earlier research on brown bears had indicated that from 31 to 79 percent of salmon (depending on the site) were killed by bears, but only about 10 percent of the fish perished before they had a chance to spawn. This bounteous supply of high-nutrition food enabled brown bears to build up an adequate fat reserve during the brief Alaskan summer and endure the long dormancy of winter. Frame wanted to find out if the black bear's impact on salmon was similar to the 10 percent, before spawning, taken by brown bears.

It was an exciting and absorbing summer's work for the young biologist. The area around the salmon-spawning stream had been uplifted about 5 feet by the great Alaskan earthquake of 1964. Olsen Creek was surrounded by a tidal flat of low-growing vegetation that made wildlife viewing easier than from along more brushy streams, which are most common in southeastern Alaska.

During the study, 26,000 chum (or dog) salmon and 27,600 pink (or humpback) salmon returned to the visible portion of Olsen Creek after several years at sea, to spawn and die. In early July, two weeks after the first salmon appeared, the first black bear arrived and began fishing. Several more bruins arrived during the next week. After that, until mid-September, most or all of the identified black bears fished every day. Frame noticed during the eight weeks that the salmon were numerous and easy to catch, and the bruins fed on almost nothing else.

Frame also noticed that most of the fishing bears were juveniles and young adults, which he could identify by physical features such as sex organs, size, scars, color and condition of coat, shape and color of chest patches, even the color of the muzzle and eyebrows. No brown bears fished in Olsen Creek, although they were observed fishing in another brook only a mile away. Frame figured that the larger male black bears were more secretive and stayed away from the tidal part of Olsen Creek next to the Pacific Ocean. Also, some of the largest adults had probably been shot by hunters.

Because Olsen Creek was fairly shallow and clear, the bears fished by running upstream in the cold water, catching a salmon, and killing it with a crunching bite. Not every "charge" was successful, and an inexperienced bruin might have to do a lot of running to catch a fish. Not all salmon were eaten, or eaten entirely. Thin ones, nearly "spawned out," were dropped immediately. Often only the eggs and a small amount of

Black bears each have recognizably different facial characteristics, as well as differently colored pelage. They tend to become heavier in the jowls with maturity. These bears and the bear on page 38 were photographed from an elevated blind, over bait, with a long telephoto lens.

flesh of the unspawned chum salmon were eaten. It is a habit that may seem wasteful, but all of the salmon is eventually recycled. I have seen gulls, Steller's jays, crows, ravens, bald and golden eagles, red foxes, and even wolves feed on parts of salmon bears have discarded.

Frame noticed that on certain days, the bears did not chase and capture live fish, but ate dead, abandoned ones instead. The Olsen Creek bears also had a definite eating procedure. After carrying the salmon ashore, they commonly used their teeth, claws, or both to rip open the body cavity and spill the pink eggs onto the ground.

Frame also had ample opportunity to study interactions between bears on Olsen Creek. Inevitably one bruin would try to take a fish from another, or simply approach too close to a fishing area already taken. Usually these confrontations would end in the two bears standing face to face, giving a series of rolling, screaming grunts. Less often they might growl or emit a catlike, snarling whine. The face-off usually ended when the aggressor bear chased off the other for a short distance.

On one occasion Frame observed a brief fight between two black bears. It began when both bears stood up, grunting and urinating simultaneously. They swatted at each other with forepaws and then circled each other like boxers, about 9 yards apart. The contest ended almost as suddenly as it began when the two lay down a few yards apart and fed on salmon carcasses. On the whole, however, those black bears had a fairly peaceful fishing summer.

Unlike the brown bears of Alaskan salmon rivers—which tend to fish in individual and rather small territories (beats) or fishing holes—the Olsen Creek blacks did not restrict themselves. All seemed to have the run of the entire creek. When actually fishing, a black would, on average, capture a fish on every third attempt. Frame estimates that the 18 bears he studied removed 2,240 unspawned salmon in all from the creek during eight weeks. About the same number of unspawned males were caught, but not eaten. In other words, the bears fished about 8 percent of the salmon that entered Olsen Creek to spawn. Thus, it appears black bears are not serious predators of salmon.

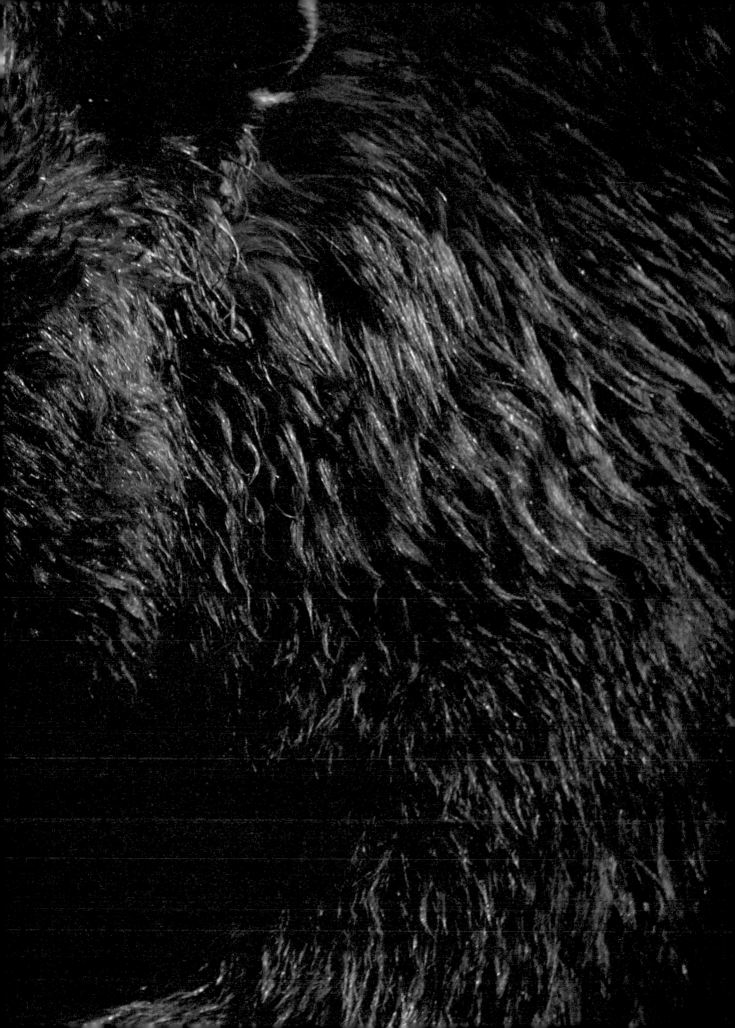

Nuisance bears often become quite bold, moving to food sources in broad daylight. Many, however, prefer the protection of darkness.

Like all of the world's bears, a North American black may at first seem slow and clumsy afoot. But that is deceptive, because the fastest human could not begin to match an adult bear's speed over rough terrain.

NUISANCE BEARS

Many of the most interesting bear stories—as well as bear theories—concern the high intelligence of black bears. Typical is the one about a boys' summer camp in central Quebec where a black bear, which the staff and young campers called Oscar, began to frequent the camp garbage dump. At first the bear was fun to watch, but gradually it grew bolder and bolder until it became a dangerous nuisance. This happens all too often in outlying areas where people feed bruins because they enjoy seeing them, and then find they have a demanding guest on their hands. A bear that has become accustomed to easy handouts is hard to drive away. That was what happened at the boys' camp. They realized they had to get rid of the bruin, but wanted to do so without killing it.

Conservation officers were called to remove Oscar. One ranger, who had considerable experience with bears, built the kind of cage bear trap with trap door that had worked well for him in the past. It was baited with walleyes (often called walleyed pike), which the animal especially liked.

The first evening, the bear arrived on schedule, approached the cage, sniffed the fish inside, and then sat down without going in. Sniffing again and licking its lips, the bear seemed to be in deep thought, as if it knew something was wrong. Then, almost as if trained to do so, it walked around to the rear of the cage, and shook it just enough to spring the trap. The door slammed down with Oscar still outside. But he was now able to reach inside, scoop out the walleyes with a paw, and carry them away.

There is a sad ending to the story about Oscar. Although a number of other clever trapping devices were eventually set, including one of

Pages 42 and 43: Where the ranges of the two overlap, black bears and gray wolves coexist without confrontation, going their separate ways. But occasionally there may be disputes over food, usually the carcass of an animal. Whether bear or wolves win depends on the size and determination of the bear, the number of wolves, or on which animal "owns" the carcass.

the tried-and-true culvert traps, nothing fooled Oscar. One night he broke into the camp kitchen and among other viands, guzzled a gallon of cooking oil used to deep-fry fish. He may also have carried away the cook's Siamese housecat because it was never seen again after that night. On his next visit, Oscar was shot dead.

Some bears we have met or heard about from reliable sources actually seem able to reason. Many a hunting guide has learned, for example, that once a bruin is chased and treed by dogs, and it somehow manages to escape, the animal understands that taking refuge in a tree is unwise. Thereafter it will continue to run, rather than climb, and many a pursuing dog has been killed or badly injured when it finally "caught" the bear.

Maybe the most intelligent—perhaps even calculating—bear I ever heard about lived in Great Smoky Mountains National Park, where numerous black bears can be a nuisance to hikers on the high hardwood trails. To be careless with trail foods, especially at night, is asking for trouble. Any backpack not meticulously cached is likely to be ripped open and the contents consumed. Tennessee bears have learned well that a backpack and food are synonymous. As a result, hikers there and elsewhere are advised to hang their packs from stout tree limbs some distance from camp, and with the packs suspended high enough above ground to be out of reach of the tallest standing bears. Done properly, this does foil bears. All except one.

One night a bear climbed into a tree on which a few bulging backpacks were hanging. It walked out onto the limb and, we might even suppose, studied the packs hanging below just out of reach with their candy bars, granola, dried fruit, and cereal. So near, but yet so far. Next the animal launched itself into the air, grasping the backpack on the way down. The sudden impact of its 300 pounds snapped the nylon rope. The bear enjoyed a delicious midnight snack on the ground. In fact, that same bear, which was named the Deep Creek Leaper, after its locale, perfected its technique and rarely muffed an attempt.

In Yosemite National Park, bears learned how to operate a complicated cable and pulley system devised to store backpacks out of their reach. Another preventive measure being tested for food storage is a completely enclosed cyclone fence cage located in popular camping areas.

Great Smoky Mountains Park rangers have long been confronted with the usual summer problem of bears panhandling beside the highway and loitering around litter depositories. One season they tried using baseball bats and found these effective for a time. The bears simply did not like being bopped on the nose, and the worst offenders seemed cured of their bad habits. But eventually the animals were able to recognize a ranger's green uniform, and simply hid until the people with the bats drove away. They could distinguish between humans who were likely to feed them and those intent on whacking their noses.

Some evidence suggests black bears may have expanded their ranges within national parks to places where they had been unable to survive before the arrival of so many backpackers and backcountry travelers. Yosemite biologist David Graber, who began studying black bears in 1974, is convinced that human use of the National Park's high country attracted bears to higher alpine reaches. He believes that bears are now able to survive above 8,000 feet or so, because the granola and beef jerky they can scrounge has the protein their natural diet chronically lacks.

A similar situation may exist in Great Smoky Mountains Park, where many of the 400 or 500 resident black bears have developed a taste—if not a craving—for campers' foods. Day in and day out during the summer tourist season, chocolate bars require less hunting effort than licking up ants and ground beetles or digging out wasp nests.

The Deep Creek Leaper I mentioned earlier may have been the most spectacular Smoky Mountain bruin, but others are just as inventive and successful. According to Stuart Coleman, a park official, some bears have taken to lurking around sunny forest glades where hikers pause to rest along the steep Appalachian Trail. Once a hiker slips out of his sweaty backpack harness and stretches weary muscles, a bruin rushes from the underbrush, seizes a pack, and makes away with it. A loss like that can abruptly end a pleasant summer holiday.

One female bear "worked" the Siler's Bald area of the Great Smokies. This one lurked near a park-built shelter, and when people went inside, the bear trapped them there by circling outside in an intimidating manner. The campers, thus besieged, would feed the bear in hopes she would go away. But this only reinforced the bruin's aberrant behavior.

In a more common tactic, a bear would simply confront hikers walking along a trail with bluffing, by woofing and snapping its jaws. The typical hiker had never encountered any bears before, let alone an aggressive one, and often shed his pack to run away faster. Of course that was exactly what the bear wanted. According to a ranger: "Our bears have sampled every kind of candy bar manufactured in the United States. And they prefer all of them."

Ralph Richardson of Marinette, Wisconsin, a veteran warden with the Wisconsin Conservation Department, had plenty of problems and frustrations during 16 years of working with "intelligent" black bears. Late one summer afternoon he was called by a nearby farmer to investigate a sheep kill. Richardson left immediately and arrived about dusk, and he was met by the farmer and his 13-year-old son. They took him to a dead sheep, which was about half consumed.

"Because of the late hour," Richardson said, "and since I had no traps or gun in the car, I told the farmer I would be back in the morning. Besides, the bear had probably eaten its fill and wouldn't return for awhile. No sooner were the words out of my mouth when the kid was hollering, 'Here he comes!'"

The farmer turned and raced toward his house for a rifle. But before he could return to use it, the bear was gone with the rest of the sheep carcass.

What followed is another rather typical account of a bear driving grown men crazy. Bear traps were set by Richardson in likely places around the farm, but by the third day they had caught only two of the farmer's dogs and a 350-pound swine. The bruin left plenty of footprints around the traps, but merely expanded its sheep killing to neighboring farms. Warden Richardson then requisitioned an old bear-hound called Nemo. The dog found the hot track easily, but after a short run, Nemo soon disappeared in a swamp of the Wolf River. So much for the hounds.

Now desperate, Richardson and fellow wardens built platforms in the woods and put irresistible (he thought) bear bait around them. A fishing line was rigged to the bait from one platform so that even in pitch dark the armed men on vigil would know when the bear arrived and started feeding. They also rigged a floodlight, which could be switched on to illuminate the bruin. One night Richardson could hear the bear coming slowly and cautiously. He thought he could even smell it on the warm, damp night air. Soon it was only about 16 feet away and almost directly below. Richardson felt a light tug on the string. He could hear the bear breathing now. In a minute....

The warden switched on the light, but no bear was on the scene. Apparently it had only brushed the fishing line, realized something was wrong, and turned and vanished. The wardens went home to catch a few hours sleep. But when they returned next morning, the bait was gone. The phantom bear had struck again.

A week later, after still more wardens and volunteers were on the job, the 360-pound male was finally killed. Both its front feet were crippled, probably from previous encounters with traps. That bear had learned a lot about human devices, but not quite enough.

That summer, Richardson and his colleagues had to kill seven bears, all males, in the Argonne and Crandon areas of Wisconsin. One of these proved to be a very hard case.

A logger east of Argonne had set up housekeeping for the summer in timberland where he was busy cutting wood. He bought a cow and calf, which he installed in an old barn. The first night the animals were in their new home, a bear tore a hole in one wall and killed both. It appeared that the cow was dispatched with a single, terrific blow. Claw holes near the head of the animal were the only marks. The bruin ate the cow's udder and part of the calf, leaving both carcasses in the barn.

Richardson set a large bear trap in a small entrance about 2 feet wide and 3 feet high on one side of the barn. He also nailed up all other possible entrances, including the place where the bear had entered the night before. The warden was reasonably certain the culprit would come

Black bears ordinarily are not serious predators of whitetail deer. But in early summer, newborn or very small fawns are vulnerable to any bruins that happen along and find them. A few individual bears may actually hunt for fawns.

back and be caught, having only one way to enter. The bear came back, all right, but it wasn't caught. Rather than use the one easy entrance, the bear ripped out another whole section of wall. After eating its fill of the cow, the bear decided to take the carcass of the calf, and exited through the 2 × 3 foot hole it was supposed to enter. But the calf's carcass set off the trap as the bear carried it in its mouth. Richardson had the calf, but still not the bear.

The warden eventually bagged the black bear, a large male of 400 pounds. But I can easily understand how, by the end of autumn, he had come to believe that black bears have human intelligence. A good many conservation officers across America have had similar or worse troubles attempting to dispose of nuisance bears. And not all these bears were caught or shot. There are many records of problem bears simply disappearing, never to be heard from again. Such bears become temporary nuisances when wild food is scarce. But it is unlikely that a camp-robbing or cattle-killing bear would suddenly change its habits. The bears probably just move to a new locale.

Bears are subject to addiction, not only to domestic livestock. Tim Burton, a wildlife biologist in northern California, has much experience trapping bruins, more to gather scientific information than to remove a nuisance. Burton learned that canned cat food covered with marshmallows and strawberry jam was one bait few black bears could resist. One female bear became so addicted to this concoction that she was captured nine times. Contrast this individual to all the bears that couldn't be trapped at all. One day Burton released this addicted sow from his trap only to have her crawl into the back of his pickup, looking for the strawberry jam jar. He figured it was time, after that, to conduct his trapping elsewhere.

HOMING ABILITIES

Live trapping and transporting to a distant place is a common method of removing offending bears

I photographed this yearling from my tent in a hunting camp in 1975. It was trying to drag away the head and skin of an elk, just discarded, after I had quartered the bull and had hung the meat in nearby trees to cure. Like many other black bears, this one eventually became a nuisance around camps.

from around campsites and possible confrontations with humans. But even if the trapped bears are transported to a different locale by truck, boat, or helicopter—even drugged—many have an absolutely uncanny ability to find their way "home"—often in a surprisingly short time.

A Montana bear that had lived beside a park garbage dump was captured, tranquilized, and carried about 55 miles away to the opposite side of the Continental Divide by helicopter. It was back at the dump in a week. In Michigan, a black bear was taken almost 100 miles away and released. That one was shot by hunters a month later, not far from its original capture site.

Once when working in Yellowstone Park in my youth, a troublesome bruin was caught alive near Fishing Bridge. We loaded the bear into a boat and motored from the north to the south end of Yellowstone Lake, a distance of about 35 miles. Next morning the bear was back sniffing around at Fishing Bridge. Simply stated, black bears have a remarkable homing instinct.

The average home range of a male black bear

nationwide is estimated to be 30 to 40 square miles. A female may spend a vagabond life in an area of no more than 10 square miles. Home ranges vary from larger to smaller, depending inversely on population density. Biologists who have tracked bears believe they sleep in a different spot every day—or night. This contrasts sharply with deer, which have definite bedding areas they often use over and over. Bears move constantly within home ranges in an incessant search for food or, seasonally, sex. Where hunting pressure is heavy, black bears tend toward more nocturnal lives.

RESEMBLANCE TO PEOPLE

Black bears are similar to people in more than just their sweet tooth, and their cunning, piggish, and predatory ways. The carcass of a bear that has been skinned looks eerily like that of a man. Both bears and men stand on their hind legs. A bear's spinal column and internal organs are similar to those of a man. Bears have the same kind and size of stomach. Bears are sometimes intelligent enough to solve problems with cause-effect relationships. Both humans and bears defend what belongs to them, and both are usually judicious enough to retreat when necessary. But bears are not as homicidal as some *Homo sapiens*.

In 1960, officer Ed Murray of Dayton, Ohio, was ejected (inside a capsule) from a military B58 aircraft traveling at 565 mph at 20,000 feet altitude. He landed safely near Edwards Air Force Base, California. But that was possible only because in an earlier test, a young black bear was hurled into space from the same plane at 44,880 feet, going almost twice as fast. The bruin rode to earth in its aluminum capsule, via parachute, and was none the worse for the trip. My guess is that the Air Force has probably used other black bears in spaceflight tests and in rocket-powered sleds designed to test bodily reactions.

As predators

Black bears are solitary mammals that wander all their lives over lonely tracts, mostly just to find enough food to live. This is true despite the incidents that make the most interesting retelling and reading. I have met many bears while backpacking, fishing woodland streams, or picking berries. To date, every one has promptly left the scene. I've never met an aggressive black bear. It would be a mistake to regard the species as a menace to man or harmful to other game animals. Some do hunt for ground squirrels and other creatures. But meat is rarely a large part of the average black bear's diet. Once again, however, the exceptions are the most fascinating.

John Hansen, who lived near Rhinelander, Wisconsin, spotted a fox den one spring afternoon while collecting mushrooms. He sat on a knoll for a long time and watched four fox kits play-fighting in the sun at the mouth of the den. It was the kind of idyllic tableau that made him forget about everything else. While studying the kits through his binocular, he saw all of them suddenly tumble underground for no apparent reason. But in the next instant, a sow black bear with a very small cub appeared. According to Hansen, the sow sniffed the ground for a moment and then began to dig furiously, scattering earth in all directions.

Once the sow stopped, bewildered, and looked as though she might give up. But abruptly she began to dig again, even more furiously than before, until her body was half hidden in the widening hole. She emerged eventually with a fox kit in her mouth, and immediately carried it out of Hansen's view. Her cub followed right behind, having learned a lesson.

According to tests, a black bear can run 30 mph. And compared to a man of similar size, any bruin is extremely powerful and agile. But black bears just aren't built or equipped to catch other creatures healthy and mature enough to take care of themselves. Occasionally, a very hungry bear might bite off more than it can chew. Consider the incident related by Jack D. Conley, once a fisheries supervisor for the Wyoming Game and Fish Department.

Conley and an assistant fisheries worker, Floyd Evans, were working one springtime at a trout-spawning camp at Surprise Lake in Sublette County. While collecting fertile eggs to transport to a state hatchery, Evans heard a pitiful squealing and looked up to see a black bear dragging a moose calf in its mouth. Almost immediately, an adult cow moose appeared directly in the path of the bear. The cow tried to jump on the bear's back, it seemed, to strike with both hoofs. The bear then dropped the calf and turned on the cow. At this point, Evans shot the bruin with a .300 rifle, and the bear ran about 40 feet before collapsing.

Evans and Conley thoroughly searched the scene of the encounter, where the ground was somewhat torn up. The men found no trace of either adult or calf moose, and they figured that the calf might have survived. They believe that the calf was only three days old. The bear weighed 350 pounds and measured 6 feet 9 inches, lying on its back, nose tip to tail tip. The moose cow had inflicted a deep gash in the bear's shoulder with her hooves, and Conley believes she would have driven the bear off without Evans' help.

Hibernation and denning

Early in the 1950s, when most of Michigan's Upper Peninsula was still an evergreen wilder-

Top photo: Deep swamps still offer some sanctuary for black bears in the Southeast. But timber cutting, channelization, and drainage are eliminating many of these final refuges. A black bear's mating season generally begins when bear grass (above) illuminates slopes of the northern Rocky Mountains and when pink moccasin flowers (right) begin to bloom in the northern Midwest.

Using a radio tracking device, biologist Lynn Rogers snowshoed to these black bears denned under the roots of a deadfall. On the snow and standing directly over the radio transmitter collar (not visible) on the sow, Rogers could hear the faint squealing of these cubs. He moved about 5 feet distant, dug straight down into the snow, and then tunneled to the bears. After taking this photo, Rogers replaced the snow.

ness, I happily spent a lot of time exploring the region during all seasons. This was splendid country for a naturalist or for any serious hunter to roam.

One late December morning, Lew Baker and I were hunting snowshoe hares in a snowbound forest. I could hear two eager beagles in full cry on a hot trail in the distance. Suddenly the chase turned my way and I climbed on top of a huge, old deadfall for a better shooting position. Once I was atop the trunk, something caught my eye just below me in the exposed mass of roots. First I saw the faintest wisp of steam, and then realized I was looking into the dark muzzle of a black bear. During a lifetime of almost bear-like wandering, this was the first and only time I have ever stumbled upon an occupied black-bear den. Without waiting to see what the bear would do, or where the beagles would drive the white hare, I hastily left the spot.

Later, Lew and I returned together and found, from the track in the soft snow leading elsewhere, that the bruin had moved to a new den. Until that day, both of us believed that where the mercury plunges to rock bottom, as in northern Michigan in winter, black bears could be expected to hi-bernate totally for the duration.

Black bears are now considered hibernators by biologists, even though their body temperatures, respiration, and heart rate do not drop as low as that of some other hibernators. In the den, a black bear's body temperature drops to about 88° F from a normal summer body temperature of 100–101°. The respiration rate drops about 50 percent, and other normal functions diminish by 45 to 50 percent. A bear can survive winter in a den without eating, drinking, defecating, or urinating. In fact, urine made by the kidneys is reabsorbed through the urinary bladder into the bloodstream. A bear can also be awakened, sometimes easily. How soundly the animal slumbers may depend on the thickness of the fat layer it acquired while feeding during the previous autumn, or on other factors not yet understood. Some speculate that a bear may sleep more soundly when fat supplies are low in order to survive through the winter. Late in the winter, as snow melts in promise of springtime, bears move in and out of dens uncertainly, never traveling too far away.

Dens can be in a variety of places. In the North, where a long sleep is the rule, virtually all are underground—in small caves, crevices or

Black-bear cubs stay close to their mother while very young, but range farther away as they grow up.

geological features, or beneath deadfalls or blow-downs. Clear-cutting of forests, described earlier, eliminates a lot of bear wintering sites. Dens have been found in culverts and even in abandoned mines, and beneath old vacant trapper's cabins and cow camps. Few are evident even to anyone passing close by, although melting or yellowing snow around an entrance may be a giveaway. Some bears excavate to form a large, more snug sleeping space; others apparently do no digging at all. Some (most females and some males) also carry dry grass or similar bedding material into the den. This gives extra insulation from the ground, especially important to cubs that are born in dens when their mother is sleeping and the temperature outside, directly above, may be sub-zero.

Even in the southernmost parts of their range, black bears may hibernate, or at least remain very sluggish, for a period when food is most scarce. In Florida, bears have been found sleeping above-ground in the cavities of very large trees. One animal was found sleeping in an outbuilding of a turpentine-collecting camp. Southern bears seem

Black-bear cubs learn early to seek safety in trees.

to drift in and out of a lethargic state, depending on the weather and availability of food.

BREEDING AND CUBS

Most female black bears first mate at 3½ or 4½ years old, although in an ideal environment their first mating may take place at 2½ years. Where food is scarce a female may not mate until she is 7½ years old. The sows breed every other year as long as they live, unless cubs are lost when very young; then the interval may be only one year. Usually a sow has twins, but she may produce as many as five cubs, all at birth blind and totally helpless. Each newborn weighs only ½ to 1 pound or so, which is the weight of a brown rat. In Pennsylvania and much of the rest of their range, bears give birth surprisingly early in the winter, often in mid-January. That means the cubs must snuggle in the mother's fur for two months or more before they finally blink in the light of the outside world.

While in the winter den, cubs gain their eyesight and mature slowly, building strength on their mother's milk, which is much higher in solids, total fats, and proteins than the milk of cows or many other mammals. Unlike many other mammal babies, black-bear cubs are somehow able to follow their mother full time when she finally emerges from the den. Perhaps that is why the female does not immediately begin to wander after emerging from hibernation. Instead, sows and other bears—except mature males—move only sluggishly at first, nibbling on whatever green new foods are easily available; the cubs tag close behind. Once in May in Yellowstone Park, I saw a female black bear carrying one cub in her mouth while another followed at heel.

Different kinds of disasters might befall cubs, although most sows are fierce protectors. In 1950, a cub weighing about 8 pounds was rescued from the black debris of a fire in the Lincoln National Forest in New Mexico. The cub's paws were seriously burned, so a ranger took it home to raise it and help it recuperate. The cub was named Hot Foot Teddy by the family.

This cub has climbed a white birch to escape the supposed threat of my camera.

Although black bears climb to escape danger, they also appear to climb just for the fun of it, as shown here and on the next pages.

Hot Foot Teddy was a hotshot from the start, refusing to be handled by humans, snarling at all, terrorizing a family spaniel three times as large. In time the family had to give Teddy up and send him to the Washington National Zoo. This was a good move all around. Teddy was renamed Smokey and was given U.S. Congressional protection with the Smokey Bear Act of 1952. Thus, a burned cub became the symbol of forest-fire prevention in America. Smokey lived to be 30 years old.

Some cubs remain with the mother for 1½ years, suddenly becoming independent and drifting away during their second spring, at about 17 months old, when mother drives them off. Until then, they do whatever the mother does and eat what she eats. They learn what is dangerous, where and how to find food. Some biologists believe that older, more experienced sows are much better mothers, which in various ways do not hesitate to discipline errant cubs by growling and even swatting them if they stray. The cubs of a female that loiters around a garbage dump or freeloads from tourists will also make this a career, too often with an unhappy ending.

VANDALISM SYNDROME

In his fine book, *North American Big Game Animals*, Byron Dalrymple writes that black bears may have, or in time may develop, a "devil-may-care" vandalism syndrome. They appear to take some perverse pleasure in simply wrecking anything that comes handy. A black bear can turn a clean campground or a woodlands cabin empty of food into a shambles, although the bear is probably motivated more by hunger than by perversity. Still, there is reason to wonder.

For several years, Peggy and I had been photographing the courtship antics of ruffed grouse on a certain drumming log we found near our home in Wyoming. Without fail for three years running, male grouse came to this specific fallen tree trunk in late May to perform their courtship ritual. So we built a hasty blind of aluminum rods and a canvas wraparound sheet. We sat behind the sheet on old kapok-filled boat cushions and aimed telephoto lenses through slits in the canvas, maintaining our grouse vigil.

At daybreak one morning we hiked to our drumming log in preparation for the final "shoot" of that season. But our blind had been destroyed. The canvas was ripped and kapok from the cushions littered the site all around. Footprints in the lingering snowbanks all about the site betrayed the culprit to be a black bear. It had also defecated near the spot.

Why did the bruin demolish our blind? The only reason we could imagine was that small, dried bloodstains from a deer killed several years before were on the canvas. Nothing more. Maybe this motivated the bear. But why did the bear also tear apart the boat cushions?

One of the countless interesting aspects of our long experience with black bears is that we'll

In a pinch, a cub may escape up the nearest tree, even if it's a small, pliable pine.

never really know them for sure. Among other things, black bears are unpredictable. They are also more intelligent and more calculating (if that is the proper word) than the other, larger American bears.

During the 1950s, before Alaska became a state, the late Frank Dufresne was chief officer for the U.S. Fish and Wildlife Service in the territory. He spent a lifetime living with bruins and eventually wrote a splendid book, *No Room For Bears*, which is packed with lively anecdotes. One of them takes place at a lonely cabin near Fairbanks, which was also an illegal whiskey still.

One day, a black bear broke into the cabin and celebrated by swilling a large amount of fer-

mented mash. Next it broke open a keg of molasses and apparently rolled around drunkenly in the thick syrup. At the same time it knocked over a stovepipe and clawed open a down sleeping bag. At that point, the moonshiner returned to his shack and opened the door. Tarred, feathered, and probably terrified, the bear crashed through a closed window and escaped into the forest wearing the window frame around its neck. A friend asked the moonshiner why he didn't shoot the bear.

"Bullets would never have stopped that thing I saw," he answered.

CHAPTER 2
GRIZZLY BEARS

Grizzlies often rise on hind legs to get a better view of things, not—as some hikers might contend—just to scare you.

Natural historians have long pondered the identity of the first European to encounter the remarkable American animal and legend we call the grizzly bear.

Almost certainly it was a member of the expedition of either Cabeza de Vaca or Francisco Coronado in about 1540. Both of these Spanish explorers wandered widely over the American Southwest in search of golden cities heaped with treasures that existed only in their dreams. Thus, the first grizzly ever killed by a non-Indian was likely the victim of a bolt from a Spanish crossbow.

Over millenia, the Indians of North America, from the Sierra Madre of Mexico north to the Yukon Flats, achieved a kind of armed truce with the bears that shared their lands as equals. Most tribes attributed great cunning, immense strength, and mystical powers to grizzlies. There were bear cults and bear clans. Some regarded grizzlies as reincarnated warrior-ancestors. Indians, especially young men, would occasionally hunt grizzlies, but with their crude spears and bows it couldn't have been a healthful sport. A necklace of grizzly bear claws was medicine powerful enough to be proudly worn, and sufficient to claim a seat in tribal councils.

Physically, even a young grizzly can outperform a powerful man. The bruin can run much faster, swim better, and survive longer in colder water, and its reflexes are appreciably faster. A bear can move silently and with a stealth that was uncanny

What does a grizzly do when it discovers a cameraman nearby in its world? Perhaps nothing at all. This one seemed mildly curious for a while.

even to Indians, who could be silent and stealthy themselves. The grizzly's musculature and vascular system—with its unusually large heart and aorta—made this bear difficult to kill until modern, high velocity weapons came along. Grizzlies are able to survive terrible injuries, wounds which would kill a man. The bears had little to fear from primitive weapons and even less reason to run from humans, until the European newcomers began to settle the West.

A full grown grizzly can weigh 1,000 pounds, although an average one encountered anywhere today would be closer to half that, or less. But a grizzly of any weight can take care of itself. Elk skulls and horse's backs have been fractured by a single forepaw blow. The grizzly's jaws are hinged by two great muscles, which permit shredding and grinding of almost any bone small enough to fit in the mouth.

Keep these statistics in mind, too: A grizzly would probably defeat the world's fastest human by 30 yards or so in a 100-yard dash. A grizzly standing, say, 150 yards away, would need only 10 seconds to be on top of you, if it wanted. Luckily not many do.

Grizzlies and humans seem to have much in common, which may account for the mystique

about grizzlies that has lingered to this day. The bear's ability to rise on its hind legs is man-like. So is its torso when stripped of skin and hair. Although not as dexterous as a human, a grizzly can rotate its forearm well enough to use its front claws almost as fingers for grasping and holding. More than one ancient Indian legend tells how grizzlies led humans to new kinds or new sources of food. These legends undoubtedly contained truth, because Indians of western North America were hunters and gatherers.

FRONTIER ACCOUNTS

Now historians believe that Henry Kelsey, a literate early-day Hudson Bay trapper, was the first to describe grizzly bears in English. He reported on a "fierce and brutish type of Canadian bear" in his 1691 journals. Kelsey probably shot a grizzly, because he mentions that it provided good meat. Indians apparently discouraged Kelsey from keeping the hide because they thought it was a god.

It wasn't until over 100 years later that Americans became aware that grizzlies existed, from the journals of Lewis and Clark. Even after Captains Meriwether Lewis and William Clark completed their valiant transcontinental expedition of 1803–1806, which opened much of our northern Great Plains and northern Rocky Mountains, the official expedition records were restricted to scientists and a handful of others high in the government. Eventually tales of the formidable western bruins leaked out, and might have whetted the appetites of restless young Americans to search farther and farther westward for adventure and breathing room.

Once they crossed the Missouri River, headed toward the Pacific, the contingent of Lewis and Clark often found it hard *not* to meet grizzlies. In 1805, a grizzly chased Meriwether Lewis into the muddy Missouri. Lewis described the event in his journal:

> There was no place or means of which I could conceal myself from the monster until I could

This is the same grizzly shown above. Although mildly interested in me, it eventually wandered off without looking back.

We have found grizzly bears in distant places of extraordinary beauty, as in the foothills of the Alaska Range.

charge my rifle. In this situation I thought of retreating in a brisk walk until I could reach a tree about 300 yards below me, but I had no sooner turned myself about and he pitched at me, open mouthed and full speed. I ran into water of such depth that I could stand and he would be obliged to swim, and that I could in that situation defend myself with my espontoon.

Perhaps fortunately for the overall success of the expedition, Lewis did not have to resort to his espontoon, which is a short pike or spear. But many of the frontiersmen who followed in the wake of Lewis and Clark were not so lucky.

American frontiersman Kit Carson admitted to being treed "like a scared possum" several times by a grizzly. Jim Bridger, fur trader and mountain man, regarded grizzlies with near-awe.

Another famous mountain man, Hugh Glass, survived an encounter with a grizzly that still seems incredible today. The pulp writers of the era, most of the eastern newspapers, and even the good literary journals of the mid-1800s had a field day when Glass was mangled by a grizzly sow. Every type of publication carried some kind of account, many of them fanciful and some even

ridiculous. There was even a popular poem titled "The Song of Hugh Glass." One account of the Hugh Glass incident, written by adventurer George Frederic Ruxton, may have been most responsible for the image of the fearsome, terrifying, aggressive grizzly that persists to this day.

Ruxton interviewed a score of mountain men to write his version of the Hugh Glass bear-attack story, which appeared in 1847. According to Ruxton, Hugh Glass and a companion named Bill had been setting traps in the Black Hills of South Dakota when Glass spotted a grizzly "searching for yampa roots or pig nuts." Glass and the companion stalked the grizzly to within 20 yards and simultaneously fired muzzleloaders into the bear broadside. "The bear, giving a groan of pain, jumped with all four legs from the ground, and seeing the wreaths of smoke hanging at the edge of the brush, charged at once in that direction, snorting with pain and fury."

As Glass and companion Bill attempted to flee the bear, Glass fell . . . "and just as he rose to his feet, the beast, rising on his hind feet, confronted him. As he closed, Glass never losing his presence of mind, cried to his companion to load up

This young bear, with gray-tipped guard hairs, shows the color phase often called silvertip. The hair of grizzlies varies in color from straw or light blonde to brown (commonest) and almost black.

quickly, and discharged his pistol full into the body of the animal, at the same moment that the bear, with blood streaming from its nose and mouth, knocked the pistol from his hand with one blow of its paw, and fixing its claws deep into his flesh, rolled with him to the ground."

Ruxton continued, "The hunter, notwithstanding his hopeless situation, struggled manfully, drawing his knife and plunging it several times into the body of the beast, which, furious with pain, tore with tooth and claw the body of the wretched victim, actually baring the ribs of flesh and exposing the very bones. Weak with loss of blood, and with eyes blinded with the blood which streamed from his lacerated scalp . . . Glass sank down insensible, and to all appearance dead."

Bill, the companion, fled and later returned with a fellow trapper. According to Ruxton, "on reaching the spot, which was red with blood, they found Glass still breathing, and the bear, dead and stiff, actually lying upon his body. Poor Glass presented a horrifying spectacle: the flesh was torn in strips from his chest and limbs, and large flaps strewed the ground; his scalp hung bleeding over his face, which was also lacerated in a shocking manner."

Ruxton went on, "The bear, besides the three bullets which had pierced its body, bore the marks of the fierce nature of Glass's final struggle, no less than twenty gaping wounds in the breast and belly testifying to the gallant defense of the mountaineer."

The trappers left Glass for dead after pulling the bear off him, and relieving him of his shirt, moccasins, and firearms. They then told the rest of their trapping party that they had buried Glass. However, after some months, Glass showed up alive, though badly mutilated and in otherwise pitiable condition, at a fort some 80 miles away where he confronted his former companion with this: "'Harraw, Bill, my boy! You thought I was gone under that time, did you? But hand me over my horse and gun, my lad; I ain't dead yet by a dam sight!'"

The Hugh Glass story tells much about the nature of grizzly bears and also of the early outdoorsmen who encountered them.

Next pages: As Peggy and I sat quietly, this grizzly mother waded across Toklat Creek, leading three cubs, one of which is out of the photo. It was a twilit fall scene I will never forget.

Another bear story received wide circulation in the West in about 1830. It concerned one Joe Meek—or Markhead, according to some accounts—a newcomer to the beaver trapping community in the northern Rockies. Meek was young and brash and had not yet met a grizzly closer than rifle range. One day he followed a large bear into a thicket, boasting he would kill it with nothing but his belt axe. When Meek did not return, his companions found him severely wounded but still breathing, part of his face and all of his scalp completely separated from his body. The bloody belt axe was in his hand, but no bear was in sight.

Like Glass, Meek (or Markhead) somehow recovered; but from his eyebrows back to the nape of his neck, he was as hairless as a glacial boulder in a mountain stream. After the story of his scalping circulated from Jackson Hole to the Flathead country, people began to give grizzlies a wider and wider berth. Or, they simply shot all bears on sight. "The only bear one may trust," a member of a trapping party wrote to his mother in Pennsylvania, "is a dead one."

It is sad that modern Americans cannot see the world of Lewis and Clark, Jim Bridger, John Colter, and Hugh Glass. Wild creatures swarmed over the Great Plains in numbers similar to those of some African savannas. The encroachment of civilization had not yet caused bears to retreat to their final mountain refuges. Grizzlies were still a plains species. Lewis and Clark found them in huge numbers, for example, in the vicinity of the Great Falls of the Missouri (near present day Great Falls, Montana), feasting on the broken carcasses of countless bison killed or drowned under treacherous cut banks and swollen waterfalls. It is revealing to note that once Lewis and Clark entered the Rocky Mountains proper, on the long trek to the Pacific, and until they returned to Montana soil, they did not mention meeting another grizzly.

THE NAME "GRIZZLY"

The name grizzly is probably derived from one of two sources: from *grisel*, an old French word meaning gray; or from the Old English *grislic*, which meant horrible or demonlike. Many of the early writers called this animal a "grisly" rather than a grizzly bear. During the period when mountain men were combing the western valleys for beavers, they referred to the grizzly as Ephraim, Old Ephraim, or Old Eph, a common name for the devil. Early on, the term "silvertip" came into use. This describes certain grizzlies very well, particularly when the sun backlights the animal's long guard hairs. Today, the grizzly bear is often known as just Griz.

By any name, the grizzly is among nature's masterpieces. It moves with a speed and rhythm, even grace, that is amazing for an animal so large. The grizzly is one of the largest land carnivores that cling to existence. Only the coastal brown bear of Alaska (which may be just a larger subspecies of grizzly) and the polar bear are greater in all dimensions. The North American grizzly is the most potentially dangerous and formidable creature that walks on four feet.

THE PHYSICAL SPECIMEN

Grizzlies tend to be as unpredictable as they are magnificent to see. For 40 years I have focused cameras on everything from African lions and black rhinos to tigers and trophy bull elephants, often at very close range. Although no grizzly has ever made even a bluff or a pass at me, I still feel more uneasy photographing them than I do other large mammals.

A grizzly is fairly easily recognized in the field. Its silhouette reveals a dished face, alert ears, a high hump on the front shoulder, and the glowing halo of reflected light from the pale-tipped hairs of its long coat. But do not depend on that silver tipping as much as on the other physical characteristics. The grizzly has a broader face than the black bear. The long, curved claws of the forepaws may sometimes be seen when the animal strides over open ground. The grizzly's actual gait is difficult to describe, except to say that it appears more confident than a black bear's. I believe I can always tell the two species apart simply by the way they walk.

Grizzlies do not exist in quite as great a range of colors as do black bears. They vary from nearly coal black on one extreme to the blonde, or Toklat, bears of Denali National Park, Alaska.

I am more uneasy photographing grizzlies than any other large mammals. Besides their strength and speed, grizzlies have hair-trigger tempers and relatively high intelligence.

Profile of a typical Canadian Rockies grizzly. Contrast this profile with that of a black bear, with its rounded forehead-muzzle.

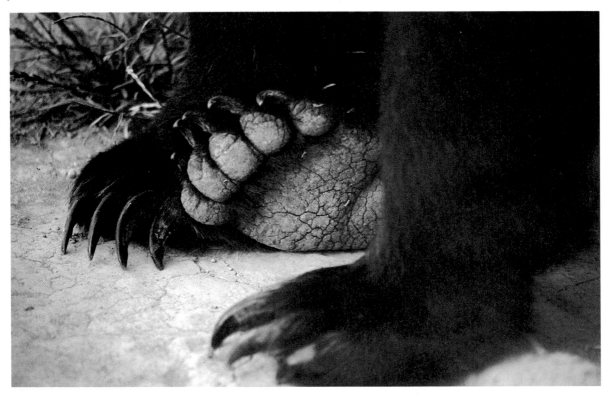

The feet of a grizzly are cushioned and padded well enough to allow rapid travel over rough terrain. Note the long, only slightly curved claws, which are not suited to climbing trees.

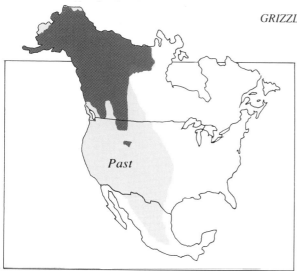

This shows the past and present range of the grizzly, which includes the range of the coastal brown bear, a grizzly master race.

But one grizzly may vary from season to season and actually seem to be several different colors, depending on the intensity and angle of the light. A bruin that is dark under an overcast sky may suddenly appear pewter-colored in a brief, temporary shaft of sunlight. Some younger bears seem to be bi-colored, with heads and legs much darker than their bodies.

DISTRIBUTION

When Columbus arrived in the New World, grizzlies existed in varying densities throughout the western half to two-thirds of what is now the United States, the western half of modern Canada, in Alaska, and in significant areas of Chihuahua, northern Mexico. But nowhere is the grizzly population more than a small fraction of what it was in 1492, or even just a century ago.

In the mid-1980s, various government agencies estimated the total grizzly bear population south of the Canadian border to be from 300 to as high as 1,000, with virtually all bears living in just three states: Montana, Wyoming, and Idaho. Nearly all of these survivors live in Glacier and Yellowstone Parks and their immediate surroundings.

VISION AND LIGHT

Grizzlies are alert and wary creatures. A grizzly's sense of smell may be more highly developed than that of most other large animals, and their hearing is good. But I have stood in full view behind camera and tripod, and had individual bears stalk right past without spotting me. Only when far enough past me, where the breeze carried my scent, did the bear stop suddenly, turn around, and try to see what it had missed. Most bear biologists, as well as most hunting outfitters I've known, do not believe that grizzly bears possess keen vision.

A large number of the countless bear-man encounters we have cataloged have taken place at night, which suggests that the species may be nocturnal. One theory is that grizzlies are diurnal, but tend to be either nocturnal or most nocturnal in areas frequented by man. That could be why they tend to prowl around campsites and garbage dumps at night, rather than in daylight. Proponents of that theory point out that most of the earliest recorded confrontations with grizzlies (as with the Lewis and Clark expedition) took place in daylight when the bears may have been disturbed when resting. The grizzlies in Denali National Park—the best place in the world to see wild grizzly bears today—are also active during daytime. Here days are long and nights are short during the season of bear activity. But as more and more people invade grizzly country everywhere, the animals may actually be evolving into nocturnal creatures. Most people find encounters with bears at night more terrifying than in daylight.

FEEDING HABITS

A grizzly can and will usually eat almost anything edible. They are definitely omnivorous, and over a lifetime they will consume more vegetation than animal food. One bear can consume a prodigious amount of low-growing berries in a summer-fall season. As often as not, the whole bush is eaten to manufacture fat reserves for the winter hibernation.

Wyoming grizzlies have been seen feeding on cutthroat trout, which spawned in small shallow feeder brooks of Yellowstone Lake. The bears also eat frozen mushrooms in fall. Biologists have watched grizzlies feeding on numerous green plants and roots growing across a mountain meadow, yet avoiding the poison death camas

Bears rise to stand on hind feet for a number of reasons, but most often just for a better look around.

The face of a large grizzly is interesting to study—when viewed through a long telephoto lens. This one is upwind of us, and is trying to get a stronger scent for positive identification.

that grew amongst the other plants. One rainy morning I watched what seemed to be an old, slow-moving grizzly turn over buffalo chips with a forepaw and lick the ground underneath, probably for the ants or grubs that it exposed. In the summer of 1951, Yellowstone Ranger Joe Way found the carcass of a mature female grizzly recently battered to death by a bison, which it may have tried to kill for food.

I once observed a grizzly eating the pine nuts from a red-squirrel cache as the squirrel circled, chattering and scolding only a few feet away. One of my most memorable experiences with grizzlies and squirrels occurred during August in Denali National Park.

A heavy late-summer snowstorm had virtually closed the park, and rangers had barricaded the single unimproved park road where the road began a narrow, winding ascent over Sable Pass. Large wet flakes were falling when Peggy and I parked our car at the barricade and discussed starting the long trip home by rough highway and marine ferry to Wyoming. If the snow continued, the park could close early and photography would

be impossible. We were feeling tired and despondent, when suddenly something moved just outside the car window. A young male grizzly, about 350 pounds and covered with snow, was staring at us from roughly 25 feet away. I quickly rolled down the window and aimed a telephoto lens at the bruin. What followed was a splendid chance to observe grizzly behavior.

A few minutes earlier, there had been a number of Arctic ground squirrels scurrying about. Now not one was in sight, but the bear began to dig into a ground-squirrel hole anyway. The deeper the bear dug, the faster its action. If the bruin heard the sound of my camera's motor drive, it gave no indication. Because the excavation site was on a sharp slope beside the road, the bear once lost its balance and tumbled to the bottom, almost against a front tire of our pickup. But it scrambled to the hole once more and dug more furiously than ever. The animal seemed in a rage because it couldn't reach the meal that it smelled—and perhaps even heard—a little farther down.

The bear dug into that and several other ground-

In summer and almost until hibernation, grizzlies feed heavily on many kinds of berries, such as crowberries (above) and blueberries (below), which are abundant in many parts of the grizzly's world. The bears often eat leaves, stems and all.

The grizzly cub at left is eating ripe soapberries (also shown in photo above) on a Toklat River bank.

As a snow begins to fall, this young male is digging for ground squirrels beside the road in Denali National Park, as described in the text beginning on page 69.

squirrel dens without success, before finally giving up and traveling elsewhere. It had expended much energy in the hunt, far more in fact than a couple of ground squirrels might have justified. I have seen other bears digging for ground squirrels elsewhere, but have never seen any bear actually capture one. On one occasion, however, I did watch twin cubs fighting over a squirrel that the mother might have clawed from the ground nearby.

In springtime, especially in Yellowstone, Montana's Bob Marshall Wilderness, and Alberta, grizzlies have been seen methodically roaming the wintering areas of elk herds in search of winter-killed elk carcasses. The bears feed on the carcasses as long as any protein remains on them. A little later they may hunt, just as methodically, in traditional calving areas for young elk that could be caught soon after birth. The spring never passes without reports of grizzlies also killing and eating mature elk, moose, and bison, though that is not common.

Despite the grizzly's considerable agility and speed afoot, it cannot consistently catch mature big-game animals in good health. And the bears seem to know it. Once late in May, from a high snowy bluff overlooking Yellowstone's Hayden Valley, I watched a grizzly walk within 30 yards or so of 24 bison without apparently even looking at them. But the bison carefully watched the bear, and turned slowly to always face it, although they did not move away from it. Later through a binocular I watched what I believe was that same bruin feeding on a winter-killed bison carcass. The bear and two coyotes remained very close to that carcass for at least the next two days.

THE VANISHING GRIZZLY

Until the mid-1960s, Yellowstone was an excellent place to watch wild grizzly bears in the early spring, beginning almost as soon as plows had cleared the main park roads of accumulated snow. It was then fairly easy to spot the animals, just out of hibernation, grazing on grassy hillsides or near animal carcasses. But no longer. The odds of seeing a grizzly in Yellowstone anywhere, anytime, are poor. But we still go looking anyway.

In May 1979, Peggy and I were approaching the south entrance to Yellowstone Park at a point where the highway roughly parallels the Snake River. We spotted large dark animals on the far side of the Snake, about 200 yards away and moving slowly in our direction. Through binoculars we immediately identified the pair as grizzly bears, probably siblings and weighing 175 to 200 pounds each. They were probably 2½-year-old cubs spending their final spring together by gorging on the lush new grass growing on that sunny slope beside the river.

Suddenly, a coyote appeared in the scene with the bears. It attacked the two head-on, biting one and then the other in the face, until the bears turned and ran in the opposite direction. The coyote continued the chase, still nipping at the bears' behinds, until the two young grizzlies paused and began slapping at one another. The coyote broke off its attack, but watched until the bears disappeared.

A 25-pound coyote routing 350 to 400 pounds of grizzly does not seem to make sense. But we soon found the explanation. The coyote was a female, and she had a den full of pups in the direct path of the feeding bears. When the bears were almost on top of the den, she flew directly at the pair, and the element of surprise turned the bigger animals around and saved the pups.

Since that day, despite much searching, we have found only one other grizzly bear in Yellowstone in the spring. Their numbers must be pitifully low.

THE CRAIGHEAD STUDY

When writing about grizzly bears, it is impossible not to write also about twin brothers Frank and John Craighead, wildlife biologists who in 1959 initiated a comprehensive study of the grizzlies in Yellowstone National Park, where the largest number still survived south of Canada. The National Science Foundation, the U.S. Fish and Wildlife Service, the National Geographic Society, the Philco Corporation, and others sponsored this now-celebrated project.

The Craigheads realized it would take radically new techniques to follow the wanderings of a wild mammal that could be active 24 hours a day, roam from horizon to horizon despite the

It is late summer and an early snow has dusted the foothills of the Alaska Range. Although a caribou bull crosses the scene, this is prime grizzly country.

roughest terrain, and sleep away half the year under some remote, snowbound windfall or cave. Thus, the brothers were the first biologists to develop and employ the then new space science called biotelemetry, using a system of radio transmitters and receivers to collect data on the bears.

During the next seven years, from 1959 to 1966, the Craigheads conducted their long-range ecological project in Yellowstone Park from a base at Canyon Village. Most knowledge of grizzlies had so far come from cattlemen or hunters looking at the animals over gunsights. The Craigheads meant to gather facts rather than prejudices. They observed the bears by practically living with them, as much as possible. And, no matter where the grizzlies traveled, the Craigheads were able to track them via electronic signals. The findings of the study were published in scientific papers and in Frank Craighead's popular book *Track of the Grizzly*.

Trapping and tagging

The study was officially under way on June 26, 1959, when the gate on a culvert trap slammed shut on an angry bear. The grizzly lunged at the trappers as they approached; it was the first grizzly they had ever seen at such close range. It looked huge, but would weigh only 200 pounds. During that first year, the Craigheads, with assistant Maurice Hornocker and several wildlife students, captured and marked 30 grizzlies with ear tags. Some were caught in culvert traps; others were taken with drug-filled darts fired at close range. Toward the end of 1960, the team had trapped 37 more bears, bringing their total of marked animals to 67 in two summers. One of those trapped and marked on July 1, 1960, was Marian, a 2½-year-old, 175-pound sow. Marked number 40, Marian would in time prove to be a very important and valuable catch.

The researchers discovered that it was possible to identify some grizzly bears fairly easily without checking the ear tags or other markers. Pegleg (number 76), for example, was named for his stiff-legged walk. The lower lip of Cutlip hung askew. Sucostrin Kid needed more than the normal dose of Sucostrin used to immobilize a bear of his size. Loverboy had a scar under one eye

Next pages: John Craighead (holding radio receiver) and brother Frank are shown in the early 1960s with a drugged grizzly outfitted with radio collar.

and was missing part of an ear. Scarface showed plenty of signs of a tough life, and the curious facial disc on Owl Face Sow reminded Frank Craighead of a short-eared owl. Owl Face was also among the first grizzly bear mothers confirmed to adopt the cubs of another female. Grizzled Sow produced a litter of four cubs, which she commanded with almost martial discipline. The longer the study lasted, the more fascinating all the subjects became.

On September 21, 1961, the gate of a culvert trap crashed yet again and this time the bruin inside was a repeater, Marian (number 40). She was quickly anesthetized and found to weigh 300 pounds, or 125 pounds more than when first trapped in 1960. She was about to become a free-roaming electronic instrument.

Radio collar

The day before, John and Frank Craighead had labored and fretted over the highly visible red-and-blue radio collar they were assembling in their Yellowstone laboratory. The collar was powered by a seven-cell battery pack, which the biologists figured would supply power for about three months. The collar weighed about 2 pounds, and it was waterproofed in silicone rubber. The men hoped that their invention, when fitted to Marian's neck, would prove to be shockproof and bearproof, as well. Frank Craighead recalls that a swirling snowstorm soon swallowed up their first radio-collared bear, revived from the drugging and released into the wild. The Craigheads couldn't help but wonder if they would ever see or hear from Marian again.

The next day was a splendid example of what makes the Yellowstone high country one of the most magnificent wild places left on earth. Bull elk were bugling in the Hayden Valley, restless Canada geese were honking and testing wings, sandhill cranes were moving up and down the Yellowstone River, as if in preparation for the long migration southward. Frank Craighead remembers hearing a coyote wail in the distance, but the sound most musical to his ears was none of these natural cries. Instead it was the high-pitched, pulsing, beep-beep-beep of the instrument in his hands. He was hearing the one par-

ticular signal which meant Marian was walking around out there—somewhere.

Not long after that, in October, the scientists made their first of many successful stalks by radio. Led by a beeping signal, louder and louder, they tramped far over sagebrush and open grasslands of central Yellowstone until they reached a prominent rise. Just below them and totally unaware of the trackers, Marian plodded along the valley floor. The radio had given the men an extra sense that surpassed even the female bear's own powers of sight, scent, and hearing. Hereafter it would be possible to track these animals as they had never been tracked before. Their lives and travels would now be open to investigation.

Habitat and behaviors

During seven years of work, the Craigheads captured 391 different grizzlies, then physically examined and recorded their pertinent data. The brothers instrumented 29 of the bears with gradually more sophisticated radio models than the first one worn by Marian. Another 212 bruins were color-marked. More than 100 of the bears were recaptured, some more than once. When forced to terminate the project suddenly in 1966, the Craigheads estimated the Yellowstone grizzly population at from 170 to 200 animals—and holding its own—despite the extent of human intrusion into the park's wild areas.

From their visual sightings of marked grizzlies, as well as by radio tracking, the Craighead brothers found the animals preferred a habitat that is a mixture of forests and open areas. Yellowstone grizzlies were not picky eaters, munching down anything from pine nuts and huckleberries to bitterroot, pocket gophers, field mice, elk, carrion, and fish. They have also been eating human leftovers at park dumps since the day in the mid-1800s when the first tourist accommodations were built in Yellowstone.

Under electronic scrutiny, the supposedly dour and lonely grizzly reveals itself as a social species. Both sexes are promiscuous. The key to life in a grizzly bear society is size, aggressiveness, and experience. The largest, oldest (if not past prime) male bear is the king of the hill. During the 1960s, grizzlies lived in all elevations of Yellowstone, but in fall moved from summer ranges to higher elevations of about 8,000 or 9,000 feet to den. Most of the dens were selected or dug, if necessary, well before hibernation. Bears wintered in the same locations year after year, if not actually in the same den.

Cubs

One to four cubs are born in winter in the mother's den. The average litter is two or three. Males outnumber female cubs two to one, but when three to four years old, they are equal in numbers. There were more females in the adult population during the Craighead study.

Almost half of all cubs born do not survive the first year and a half. Some very reclusive and durable bruins may live to 25 or even 30 years, but the average life span is only five to six years. During the Craighead investigations, almost one of every five grizzlies became a "problem bear" and had to be eliminated in the Park. Hunters accounted for a very heavy toll—about 40 percent—of those that ventured outside park boundaries where hunting was then legal. Of course, other bears die annually of old age, disease, accidents, fighting—all causes that are difficult to confirm and count.

Effects of handling

A reader may wonder how bears are affected by being trapped, drugged, handled by humans, and collared. Frank Craighead is convinced that travels and love life, family relationships, and general behavior of Yellowstone bruins were not noticeably altered by their work. Untagged, uncollared bears kept under visual observation did not act any differently than those carrying radios. But there may be some relationship between frequently handled bears and abnormal behavior. A grizzly that dragged a West Yellowstone camper from his tent (and partially ate him) had a record of having been previously handled 19 times.

Territories

One unknown fact about bears was how far they ranged, and whether they had "home terri-

tories." The Craighead study indicated that grizzlies were prodigious travelers, with males making far more footprints on the average than females. Pegleg, the bruin with the curious gait mentioned earlier, was found to have a summer range of 168 square miles. Bruno, one of the largest males tracked and studied, might have turned up in any corner of the 3,500-square-mile national park, or even outside it. Bruno had eventually been credited with a lifetime summer range of 1,000 square miles. The paths of different bears frequently cross and re-cross without conflict during their travels, which are mainly in search of food. Most of the bears in a regional population, as in Yellowstone, get to "know" one another by scent and other signs, if not exactly by sight. Each bear tries to keep a proper distance from other bears of superior rank.

Dumps

For a long time the refuse from the hotels and cabins around Old Faithful was buried at a dump beside Trout Creek, a minor tributary of the Yellowstone River. Most of the Yellowstone bruins visited the Trout Creek dump at intervals during the brief high country summer, much as Alaskan brown bears regularly visit a favorite salmon spawning stream annually to fish. The dump was in existence so long that by 1959, when the Craighead study began, it was part of the bear existence. No doubt it was the place Yellowstone bears became most acquainted with one another, and where bear hierarchies were determined.

During just one night's observation in 1966, 88 different grizzlies were present at Trout Creek. A year earlier I had counted 33 there in one night. During the 1965 summer season, 132 different grizzlies (or about 75 percent of the estimated park grizzly population) were recorded coming to Trout Creek. The abundance and in-and-out traffic of grizzlies at Trout Creek explains why

Next pages: This grizzly cub on a Toklat River bar is an orphan. In May of that year two biologists watched as a male grizzly killed the cub's mother and a sibling in a sudden violent encounter. This cub somehow escaped. But it is doubtful that the cub was able to survive the winter, alone in hibernation.

The faces of grizzlies are as different from one another as are the faces of humans. When photographing or working with bruins over a period of time, one can instantly recognize many individuals.

he recovered; but he limped and tottered nervously the rest of his life. A price of $200 was placed on Two Toes' head, the going rate for shooting any human cattle rustler.

Nobody in the Swan Valley figured they would actually have to fork over the $200 for Two Toes. Cattle killing had stopped and all believed (or wanted to believe) that Kline had fatally wounded the brute. But in the spring of 1904 the trouble started all over again. There were those maddening, unmistakable bear tracks around 29 dead calves, plus several cows and steers, in a single foray up and down the valley. According to one newspaper account, Two Toes would crush the calves' bodies with a single swipe, and not always linger long enough to eat them. Some cattle were just left for wolves (which still existed in Montana then) and coyotes to finish off. The necks of larger livestock would be broken, the ribs smashed and partially eaten, the carcass raked with long claws from end to end. For good measure, Two Toes also killed several horses in passing.

By mid-summer, the slaughter in Swan Valley abruptly stopped, only to start again a week or so later on the opposite side of the Mission Mountains. Like many of the male grizzlies radio-tracked years later by the Craigheads, Two Toes roamed over a vast summer range. But no sooner were the Swan Valley cattlemen sighing in relief, when Two Toes appeared once more. One afternoon, Caleb Myres was riding across a great meadow when he saw vultures circling and coyotes running away. Further on he spotted the limp carcass of one of his heifers, with two-toed tracks surrounding it.

The next morning Myres went riding in the same area he'd found the mangled heifer, this time with a carbine in his lap. Judging from the fresh sign all around and the nervous behavior of his horse (many of which have a keen sixth sense about the presence of bruins), Myres figured Two Toes might still be somewhere nearby. He tethered his horse to a tree and climbed to the top of a ridge for a reconnaissance. He was barely out of sight when he heard the horse squeal in pain.

Racing back toward his horse, Myres heard—and for a split second saw—a furry brown figure crashing away through brush. But now he had a long hike back to his ranch because his mount was stone dead. The head was nearly torn from the body of what had been a fine cow pony. And Myres would always be able to identify his saddle from the deep claw marks etched across the seat.

Now a new factor entered the incredible story of Two Toes. At the time, gangs of human outlaws were rustling cattle in Montana and driving them into nearby Canada. The rustlers were desperate men; many were jail-breakers. Whenever Myres, his men, and fellow ranchers went out looking for one menace, they had to keep an eye open for the other. There was even one contemporary rumor that rustlers cleverly covered their own tracks with the paw of a two-toed bruin. Altogether, 1905 was a year in which Two Toes killed cattle over an area larger than 1,000 square miles. He culminated the season by destroying two powerful stud bulls, pastured together not far from the Ferguson Ranch buildings, which adjoined Caleb Myres' spread.

The winter of 1905–1906 was one which northwestern Montana residents would remember bitterly for a long time. The snow began to fall early in September and never seemed to end. Just keeping livestock alive until spring became a monumental no-win task.

But when springtime finally came, Two Toes was back, traveling on a wide itinerary throughout and surrounding the Swan Valley that could be easily traced by the trail of dead domestic creatures it left behind. At the summer meeting of the local stockman's association, an experienced French-Canadian hunter-trapper named Henri Belieu was hired. He was guaranteed a $675 reward for killing Two Toes, a figure which would compare to about $10,000 today.

Belieu wasted no time getting started. He owned two airedales, which a reporter described as "vicious," and by a stroke of luck soon hit the trail of Two Toes where it had stalked a band of elk and killed a cow. Belieu's airedales attacked the bear, which promptly broke the back of one and split the other in half before the trapper could reach the scene. The Frenchman was so enraged at the sight of his broken dogs that he swore to kill Two Toes for revenge alone.

A few days later, cowpokes were branding

colts and when finished, turned 70 of them out of the corral to pasture. It was a routine chore. Two, Hawkey and Moore, remained with the horses while the others went down the mountain toward home. They hand-rolled cigarettes and were enjoying a smoke when they heard the familiar terrified squeal of an animal being attacked. The men jumped on their horses and rode up the creek toward the sounds. Suddenly, a huge grizzly rose up directly in front of them.

Hawkey's horse bucked wildly and threw him to the ground. Moore's mount reared into the other horse and both fell, almost on top of Moore, whose head was cut open. Hawkey's gun roared twice. Dazed, Moore found himself sitting beside a creek facing the bear out of focus on the opposite bank. He drew a .45 revolver and, with horse hoofs pounding all around him, fired point-blank at the bear. He also remembered hearing Hawkey fire again. Then all was quiet.

For a few seconds the cowboys just sat and listened for any telltale sound. Finally they stood up, looked around, and saw two dead colts and a dying mare. They also saw a blood trail that led away into dense brush. The grizzly tracks in soft earth beside the creek belonged to Two Toes, and the men were convinced that they had finally dispatched the terrible killer.

But Belieu soon found otherwise. During the late summer, he killed three grizzlies and several black bears while again following Two Toes' tracks. Belieu's resolve for revenge may have faltered once or twice when he found that the bear had circled around behind him and had probably been watching him. But Belieu persisted nonetheless, while paying a lot more attention to his back trail.

That same fall of 1906, two eastern hunters came to Montana in search of trophy elk and sheep, and hired a Missoula outfitter named George Thomas to pack them into the mountains. Thomas employed a man named Dale to assist him with the cooking and wrangling. In those days, the hunting pressure was still extremely light, and it was easy enough to quickly take two fine bull elk with six-point heads. The decision then was to move from their elk hunting camp to a much higher camp where they would be in the best bighorn sheep country. Around noon on

the day of the move, Dale was leading a string of seven heavily loaded horses along a thin, precipitous trail which was taking him toward the head of a steep canyon. Boulders were poised on the upper side of the trail, but on the other side the packer could stare down into dark eternity a thousand feet below.

Suddenly a loose boulder dislodged and spooked a horse. This brought the whole pack string to a halt in a cul-de-sac where there was no turning around. Dale looked up the bank beside him and stared into the face of a great yellow-brown grizzly.

By standing up abruptly, the bear started other rocks rolling. Horses bucked or tried to bolt in panic. One went over the edge to its death. The bear worked its jaws, clicked its teeth, and charged down the slope. Somehow Dale stayed cool amid the pandemonium that followed, and slipped out of his saddle intact, along with his then new .45/90 rifle.

The grizzly went directly for one of the horses, which gave Dale a chance to shoot. He put one bullet through the bear's ribs and into its lungs. Another broke its neck. A third ricocheted off its skull behind the left ear. All the wrangler remembered immediately after that is trembling and watching the lifeblood drain from the bear's mouth. Nobody knows what happened to Dale after that day, but he probably never had an experience to match that mix-up on the brink of a Montana mountainside.

That is how the life of Two Toes came to an end. The animal was estimated to weigh 1,100 pounds, and was judged to be 15, maybe 20 years old. It was sleek, fat and in good physical shape, although scarred and with teeth missing, probably from the escape from Ricks' trap. Two Toes' last day was very warm, and he had been sunning in a bed, perhaps drowsily awaiting the second trigger that would send him directly to a winter den. The pack horses had awakened him, and maybe he thought he was cornered.

So Dale, not Belieu, got the reward. Caleb Myres finally got to see Two Toes after the bruin was converted to an open-mouthed rug. During its reign, the animal had accounted for an estimated $80,000 to $100,000 worth of livestock at today's prices.

This grizzly of the southern Canadian Rockies may be marking a territory with claw and tooth marks on a sapling. Or, it may just be "tasting" the thin bark. Either way, it paused here only briefly.

Bloody Paws

Two Toes wasn't all that unusual for the time. Bloody Paws, whose territory was east of Greybull, Wyoming, to the summit of the Bighorns, was credited with 570 known livestock kills. He was finally shot by Buffalo Robe, a Shoshone Indian. Bandit, which terrorized Oregon's Wallowa Valley for five years, was eaten at a barbecue and barn dance where the man who killed it was presented with his $600 reward. Old Silver, after eluding Idaho stockmen and professional hunters for three years, was dispatched by a homesteader who found the bear eating a calf in a corral. Old Mose of near Canon City, Colorado, may have been the most publicized of the rogue grizzlies, no doubt because he also killed five human pursuers and thereby set a grizzly record for man-killing.

The first grizzly ever to have a substantial reward offered on its head was Red Robber of southeastern Utah. Since it lived in the dangerous Robber's Roost country of Butch Cassidy, which was long a rustler's hideout, no accurate count of its predations were kept. But the toll was well into the hundreds. When its dead carcass was examined, the body contained several old rifle balls and even an old arrowhead imbedded in the back.

The outlaw bears of the early 1900s had several things in common. All were males. All were apparently in good physical condition, though fairly old. All lived in parts of the West which, today, contain no grizzly bears whatever, though a few grizzlies still do roam the Mission Mountains where Two Toes sometimes ventured. Some may be descended from him.

LONGEVITY

Aging a grizzly accurately involves examining the annual growth rings of teeth—one reason why this is best done in a laboratory, rather than in the field. The Craigheads found some Yellowstone bears surviving into their third decade. In late 1982, Donna Lipen was hunting the east end of the Brooks Range in Alaska, and shot what appeared to be a bruin of good size for its Arctic environment. The animal was a sow with long and silky fur. But its teeth were badly worn, and it carried little body fat for so late in the year. The Alaska Game and Fish Department later aged the female at 32½ years. Even giving or taking a year or two, it is the oldest grizzly I've ever heard about.

GRIZZLY HUNTERS

Some very interesting and colorful people have become involved with grizzly bears throughout the short history of the United States. There was Ben Lilly of New Mexico, for example, who may have been the most persistent, if not the greatest, grizzly hunter of all. Roaming the lonely reaches of the southern Rockies, Lilly tracked cattle killers with an almost religious dedication. He once hunted a particularly large bruin for five years before finally shooting it. An eastern industrialist-sportsman had paid the long-bearded mountain man a salary just to find that super-bear.

President Theodore Roosevelt went grizzly hunting in Colorado in 1905. His outfitter was John Goff, who had built quite a reputation as a mountain-lion and bear guide of that period. Accompanied by a large press contingent and Western Union operators, T.R. arrived in Glenwood Springs on a special train of presidential cars. The Colorado Hotel in Glenwood became the temporary White House. Stepping from the train and glowing with gusto, Roosevelt said that he "had come to this land where the air is unpolluted with engine smoke, where men are few, where animals are many and savage, to eat bacon and cornbread again, and forget that there is such a thing as a fourth class post office." But T.R. also admitted that he did not want to return to Washington without slaying, single-handedly, a grizzly.

Roosevelt made a plea to the press: "When I come out of the wilderness, I'm fair game myself. But while I'm in there, let me be alone with the bears." With that he evaporated into the backcountry accompanied by his physician, a friend, Phil Stewart, 26 bear hounds, and a dozen mongrel terriers.

T.R. already had a reputation as an outdoorsman and big-game hunter, and in later years he

At intervals throughout the summer, grizzlies travel along the beds of central Alaska's glacial rivers, as here on the East Fork of the Toklat.

would make a long safari to East Africa. Among other things he was referred to as the "Big Moose on Pennsylvania Avenue." But this particular hunt did not go well. Wild rumors of bear encounters and mountain blizzards kept filtering from the presidential camp. One day a courier rode out with a large black-bear pelt swinging from his saddle. But the only word from Roosevelt himself was that he "was having bully sport." The hunt was cut short without a grizzly when a sagging stock market on Wall Street and T.R's Cuban malaria began to torment him. As he rode away from Colorado, the headline in the Denver Post read, "Lucky Day for the Grizzlies."

Less than 40 years after T.R.'s unsuccessful hunt, a Colorado Game Commission official reported that there were only ten grizzlies left in the state. From the late 1950s until 1979, none at all were seen, and it was assumed that the grizzly had vanished forever. Then in 1979, a hunting guide in the San Juan Mountains, who claimed that he was attacked, killed an old female grizzly under still unclear circumstances. Was this old sow he shot simply a final relic, or did a few other grizzlies still somehow survive in

inaccessible sections of the San Juans? In 1983, an extensive two-year search of the range uncovered no evidence of the bear's presence. Griz really had vanished from its last refuge south of Yellowstone.

BEAR-WATCHER ACCOUNTS

Not all of the grizzly people, fortunately, are out after old Griz's hide. Quite the contrary. There is my friend, Sam Miller, for example.

As a young biologist, Sam spent 18 years studying, marking, censusing, and living with bears in the most remote corners of Canada. He followed and worked with polar bears across the Arctic ice pack. He also studied the grizzly bears that lived along the Canol Road in western Northwest Territories. The Canol Road and oil pipeline were hastily built during the early days of World War II to carry petroleum from Norman Wells (a far north outpost on the Mackenzie River) to the Yukon and Alaska. It was a massive, emergency construction job to supply oil in case the Japanese occupied Alaska. When that danger passed, the Canol was abandoned as suddenly as it was

Though Alaska's riverbanks serve as convenient bear highways, they also provide food, such as the soapberry that ripens in August.

More than once, we have found grizzlies splashing in clear wilderness streams for no obvious reason other than to cool off.

started. Today the road—along with isolated crumbling, uninhabited camps—is only an ugly scar on the Northwest Territory landscape. The road is now impassable.

The actual toll of grizzlies during construction of the Canol is unknown, except that it was high. The animals were shot simply for the hell of it. But 30 years after the bulldozers were left behind to rust, Sam Miller found bears again living in the region. One eventually tried to evict Sam from his log-cabin headquarters by climbing into the window one night.

"If I live to be 200," Sam told me, "I'll never forget thrashing around in that pitch black room, unable to see anything, with a grizzly. Things were flying in all directions. I crawled on the floor feeling for a fallen flashlight, but my hands found a furry foot instead. Somehow in all the confusion, the bear got back out the window, and here I am."

Sam Miller has built a comfortable guest lodge on a slope overlooking the Barrens, a vast tundra punctuated with ponds and stretching away to the snowy Selkirk Mountains. He and his guests see

grizzlies (and possibly even that same one) nearby throughout the short summer and early fall, when Oldsquaw Lodge is open for business. It is by far the best place we have ever found, with the exception of Denali Park, Alaska, to see a grizzly in the wild. But it is an even better place to observe the other wildlife of that sub-arctic community at close range.

A growing number of Americans, besides Sam Miller, are absolutely militant about saving the grizzly. But none, perhaps, are more dedicated than Doug Peacock.

When Doug Peacock returned from duty in Vietnam, he had never seen a grizzly and knew nothing about them. Since then he has become a cinematographer, specializing in grizzly bears. He now has many thousands of feet of film, including some of the finest scenes of grizzly life and behavior ever taken.

Getting interested in bears, Peacock admits, was the luckiest of accidents. The way he tells it, he was soaking in a hot pool at Yellowstone one October afternoon to try to alleviate a recurring malaria attack from Vietnam. Suddenly, a sow bear with cubs walked up to him. In his fear, he scrambled out of the water too quickly and ran head-on into a tree. Somewhat groggy, he fought his way up the tree, as he described it, "leaving blood and skin on the trunk. I spent the next hour and a half blue, naked, and bleeding while the bears grazed peacefully in the meadow below, as if I didn't exist."

Peacock started reading all he could about grizzly bears. During summers as a forest ranger stationed in remote fire towers at Yellowstone and Glacier National Parks, he was able to watch bears. In his spare time, he began filming them with an old 16mm Bolex hand-wound camera. Alone and on equal footing with the grizzlies, Peacock shot remarkable and intimate sequences of grizzly life, that lecture audiences are now able to see. Each lecture is a part of one man's crusade to save an endangered species, wherever it still survives.

Peacock has focused on about 200 different bruins, but one of his favorites is an ancient boar he calls Happy Bear. A loner, like the camera-man, Happy Bear is revealed gamboling like a cub around a thawing pond, breaking through the ice and plunging into near-freezing water. There the bruin sits, shattering the ice by swinging its powerful forepaws, picking up a sliver of ice and sucking it. "Happy could play by himself for hours," Peacock says approvingly, "he seemed to be a very contented bear."

The part of Peacock's lecture film that most

Occasionally grizzlies pause to groom and scratch, and at times seem to enjoy the pause. They are often bothered by mosquitos, ticks, and chiggers.

moves audiences is the scene of bear cubs wrestling, play-fighting, and leaping upon one another as a pair of cuddly beagle puppies might do. It is play now, sure enough, but the cubs are beginning the long training necessary for survival in their adult lives.

A poignant philosophy has derived from Doug Peacock's exposure to grizzlies. It somewhat parallels the Plains Indian belief that God sent grizzlies down to make men humble. Peacock also realizes he is out of step with a nation that doesn't care whether "dangerous" animals survive.

The grizzly hierarchy is a sort of caste system, with the most dominant males at the top and the youngest or most submissive females at the bottom. A bear's rank can improve as it gains age, strength, and aggressiveness. Or an animal may lose rank with increasing age, as when a younger male ousts a once-dominant boar from the top or alpha position. Peacock believes that bears react to him as they do to other dominant individuals. They tolerate his presence and usually respect the space around where he stands, armed only with the camera.

Most bruins do not like the scent of humans and try to avoid it. Peacock even tried rolling in woodsmoke and campfire ashes, but that didn't camouflage his smell. Bears challenge one another in subtle ways as well as by obvious means, such as a stiff-legged walk or swagger, a head held at higher than normal angle, or a direct rather than a sidelong approach. They have also challenged Peacock. "When that happens," he advises, "you have to assert your dominance. You do it by standing up and talking to him."

Anyone who wanders deliberately searching for grizzlies that can be approached near enough for photography is bound to know times of terror. Throughout one night, a surly boar kept Peacock awake in a cold sweat by shuffling around just outside the tent. Although the night ended with Peacock completely exhausted, he feels the animal was only trying to tell him something. Next morning after the bear had eaten a dirty T-shirt, Peacock went elsewhere to use his camera.

Next pages: A Montana grizzly wades into a stream to cool off. Earlier, the stream offered protein in the form of spawning cuttroat trout.

This young grizzly above is digging furiously, although not too expertly, for Arctic ground squirrels. The same bear is shown at left chasing a squirrel that it flushed from an underground den.

pies—perhaps even coyotes—from farther and farther away. Somehow the grizzly was also tuned in on this raven "telegraph" system. Upon arrival, each bruin tore open the carcass, enabling smaller wildlife to join in the recycling. Frank Craighead believes that in both cases the bears demonstrated only a part of the interdependence of all creatures and plants in the ecosystem.

That interdependence can be taken much further. When changing abruptly from a mainly carbohydrate diet of grass, forbs and berries, to the proteins in big-game animal meat, rapid elimination is likely to occur. The bear will defecate frequently and copiously around the area. This leaves piles of many kinds of seeds, some undigested, which might eventually sprout as food plants for grizzlies and even for black bears. Thus, the process continues.

GRIZZLIES AND BLACKS

Do grizzlies and black bears get along? The answer is that they probably do, but by keeping to different habitat types in the same ecosystem. When in 1950 I first began spending part of almost every summer in Yellowstone Park, both grizzlies and blacks were fairly abundant. Black bears were much easier to see during the tourist season, because so many wandered and panhandled along park highways—something grizzlies seldom did.

If given the chance, a hungry adult of one species would surely snatch a cub of the other. There is an old report from Waterton Lakes National Park, Alberta, of just such an event. A grizzly was seen dragging away a yearling black bear not far from the Prince of Wales Hotel. It is entirely possible that the yearling was one of the "camp bears" that disappeared at about the same time.

Grizzlies fit very well into a niche at the top of their food chain. They thrive well until man comes upon the scene. Since Lewis and Clark, grizzly and man have been on a collision course.

BEAR-AND-BULL FIGHTS

When the Spanish first colonized southern California, they immediately developed a new bravado culture in which old Griz played an unhappy role. Instead of organizing the traditional Castilian bullfights to celebrate religious holidays, bear-and-bull fights (which were bloodier) became the popular entertainment. A grizzly bear was released into a stockade with a fierce range bull, and the two were goaded to fight it out.

The first problem was to acquire bears. Bears were plentiful enough throughout southern California, and, in fact, may have reached their greatest pre-Columbian density there. The bruins roamed from La Jolla to Laguna Beach, from Redondo to Malibu, where humans throng in the millions today.

In time, teams of vaqueros became adept at the hazardous job of capturing wild grizzlies alive with *reatas*—lassos of specially braided oxhide. The strategy was to drive a bear into the open, surround it, and, from horseback, lasso the enraged animal from four different sides all at once. With four horsemen stretching the bear in four directions, someone else slipped in, flipped the bruin on its back, and hastily shackled the bear with stout rope. The bear was then carried off in a cart to a stockade or arena.

A bull weighing as much as a ton is a formidable adversary. But according to remaining records, a bull was often no match for a grizzly in good health. What often happened, however, was that successive bulls were fed into the stockade until the bear was finally gored to death. Then as now, sentiment did not favor wild animals.

Bear-bull fights were still going on when California became a state in 1850. Recently, I examined a crumbling old poster that advertised a bear-bull fight held in Placerville, California, in about 1856. It read:

WAR !   WAR !   WAR !
the celebrated Bull-killing Bear,
GENERAL SCOTT,
will fight a bull on Sunday the 15th inst,
at 2 P.M.
at Moquelumne Hill

The bear will be chained with a twenty-foot chain in the middle of the arena. The bull will be perfectly wild, young, of the Spanish breed, and the best that can be found in the country. The Bull's horns will be of their natural length, and *not sawed off to prevent accidents*. The Bull will be quite free in the arena, and not hampered in any way whatever.

General Scott won, killing not one, but two bulls on Moquelumne Hill. But returning injured to the ring a week later, he was killed by a fresh bull.

A few bear-bull matches were held in Nevada gold camps. At least one such bloody spectacle was promoted in Last Chance Gulch (Helena), Montana, late in 1868. A trapper from the Sun River country had succeeded in capturing a bear of enormous size. Pre-fight publicity stated that the man had trouble killing enough elk and deer to feed the vicious brute. I couldn't find documentation on the outcome of the match, or if it took place at all.

THE REAL GRIZZLY ADAMS

Another kind of grizzly-bear story also originated in California. It concerned John Capen Adams, who once lived in a basement on Clay Street, San Francisco, and who walked the streets of that town followed by one or more grizzly bears. Even in 1856, a quarter-ton bear strolling the streets like a well-mannered dog still drew plenty of attention.

The real "Grizzly Adams" was born in Massachusetts where, as a young man, he worked for a circus. But he was mauled by a tiger he was feeding and, in his own words, "became disgusted with the world." There is a void in his life until 1849 when, at 42, Adams arrived in California with, he recounted, "a Kentucky rifle, a Tennessee rifle, a revolving pistol, several Bowie knives, a buoyant and hopeful spirit." In the Golden State, he got into the business of capturing wild animals.

With two Indians, Stanislaus and Tuolumne, and a Texan named Sykesey, Adams roamed the game-filled California backcountry capturing mountain lions, bears, and wolves. One day Adams came into possession of a snarling, female grizzly cub that began to monopolize his attention. Through some rare combination of stern discipline, imprinting, and animal intuition, Adams raised the cub into adulthood and total devotion to him. He named the bear Lady Wash-

ington. She followed Adams wherever he went, whether he was building traps or stalking other bears. "She was the purtiest animal I ever saw," John Adams claimed.

The time had to come when the odd couple would meet another grizzly face to face. Adams was stalking to get close enough to shoot a deer with a pistol, the only arm he carried, when he was suddenly confronted by a bruin. It probably was a male and it did not run, which was a bad sign. But Lady Washington snorted, chattered her teeth, and lunged at the other bear, which finally retreated. Grizzly Adams always credited his bear with saving his life.

When winter closed in on the High Sierra, Adams loaded up all his captured animals and headed in a strange caravan toward Portland, Oregon. There the cargo, except for Lady Washington, was put aboard a sailing bark, *Mary Ann*, bound for Boston. Adams and the lady bruin wintered in a log cabin where the bear slept fitfully under the floor most of the time.

Next spring, the trapper was back in Yosemite Valley on another expedition. Camped along the Merced River, today the site of a vast and noisy recreational vehicle park, Adams located a grizzly den belonging to a large sow with cubs. He killed the female and took the cubs alive. He decided to raise one as a companion to Lady Washington, and called it Ben Franklin. From that point onward, the man had two bruins always following him.

For reasons unclear, Adams broke camp in the Sierra and started walking eastward toward the Rockies. The three walked through Salt Lake City on the Fourth of July—to the amazement of the Mormons—and continued to Fort Bridger, Wyoming, where a permanent camp was pitched. Adams' idea was to hunt and sell meat to travelers along the now-busy road to California gold fields.

During the sojourn at Fort Bridger, Lady Washington had a romance with a wild bear that stole into camp three nights straight. But apparently the female made no great effort to break away from her captive status.

Restless and back once more in the Sierra, Adams began to trap again and caught a number of grizzlies alive, one of which, named Samson, was claimed to weigh over 1,500 pounds. He also raised other bears from cubs, but none became as amenable as Lady Washington or Ben Franklin. Eventually, Adams was badly wounded by a wild bear, and had part of his scalp ripped away. Again he credited his two ever-present "friends" with saving his life.

In 1856 injuries and fever forced Adams to give up hunting and he went public with his bruins, exhibiting them in San Jose and the California Bay area. When Ben Franklin died in 1858, the San Francisco Evening Bulletin carried a long obituary story titled "Death of a Distinguished Native Californian." Two years later, Adams took the clipper ship, *Golden Fleece*, around Cape Horn to New York City. For the first time ever, grizzly bears were seen by people of the eastern seaboard. But Adams' head had been reinjured in a struggle with one of his bears during the turbulent passage, and he never fully recovered. He died near Boston in 1870.

Even allowing for embellishment, Adams may have been the most unusual grizzly enthusiast who ever lived. He had to know many secrets of the species, and it is a shame that more of his lore does not survive.

TOWARD EXTINCTION

Like Grizzly Adams, most of the grizzlies are now gone. As Harold McCracken wrote in his book, *The Beast That Walks Like a Man*, "we have excused ourselves for subjugating the Indian and destroying his culture, and for sweeping the herds of buffalo from the plains, to make room for our farms and our towns. The best we can claim on behalf of the grizzly is that he provides a questionable menace to the welfare of domestic livestock."

Grizzlies once followed bison herds over the undulating grass prairies of Kansas, Nebraska, and Oklahoma. Nobody knows when the last one was seen, or shot, in any of those states, but it was well before the final Indian battle of Wounded Knee (1890). The last known slaying of a bear in the Dakotas was near Oakdale, North Dakota, in 1897, circumstances unknown.

Grizzlies exist in satisfactory numbers in Alberta, British Columbia, and in the Yukon and the Mackenzie District of the Northwest Terri-

tories. The species is safe so far in Alaska because of the low density of the human population.

Arizona's final grizzly fell in 1935 in Greenlee County. An epitaph marks the spot in Cache County where the last Utah grizzly died in 1923. It states that the bear stood 9 feet 11 inches tall and weighed 1,100 pounds. Its skull now sits in the dusty bowels of the Smithsonian Institution, in Washington. The last Oregon grizzly was shot in 1931 on Chesnimnus Creek, Wallowa County. Today only one complete skeleton of the California grizzly is known to exist. As late as 1916, a grizzly was caught in a steel trap in Tujunga Canyon, Los Angeles County, California. A few years before that, a grizzly was seen not far from the Rose Bowl in Pasadena. A posse went out to dispatch it. The last of a species that had thrived for a million years in California was shot in 1922 by a first-generation cattle rancher.

Man's relentless plunder of grizzly habitat and consequent eradication of grizzlies that seem to pose threats will make scenes like this rarer to come upon.

CHAPTER 3

BROWN BEARS

This brown bear suddenly looked up to stare into my telephoto lens. Once satisfied that I was no threat, the bear returned to fishing.

In 1961, Roy Randall arrived in Alaska at age 28 in search of high adventure, as so many other young men had done. He, at least, was immensely successful in finding it. Since then, Roy has led an exciting life among Alaskan brown bears.

From the time Randall arrived in the Great Land until 1972, he made a living by seal and sea lion hunting. Until then it was perfectly legal, though hard as well as often hazardous work. When commercial seal hunting ended, Randall found himself with a small plot of land at Seal Bay, a sheltered cove of Afognak Island, which was a wilderness almost totally inhabited by brown bears. Only four people lived on the island's 1,000 square miles, and none lived near Seal Bay. To Randall his place resembled Paradise, and he decided to build a modest guest lodge there for bear hunters, fishermen, and other outdoorsmen.

First Randall and his new wife, Shannon—a remarkable "city girl" who had also fallen in love with the Alaskan wilderness—built a 12 × 12-foot log cabin with logs cut by two-man saw on the spot. They didn't have the cash for a chain saw. Other materials were combed from lonely beaches and scrounged from an abandoned military barracks on Kodiak Island, 50 miles away by sea. The two planned to finance the rest of the lodge by selling the cache of seal oil Roy had collected when sealing was legal.

But one night a brown bear broke into the cache and guzzled

The faces of coastal brown bears are almost indistinguishable from the faces of inland grizzlies. But mostly because of diet, coastal bears are on average much larger.

over $500 worth of oil. Roy had to shoot the bruin that same night when it tried to climb into their small cabin, presumably in search of more of the seal elixir. The animal's coat was saturated with oil.

Somehow, working like demons, the Randalls managed to complete their project. Now their cozy, cool Afognak Wilderness Lodge has many guests throughout the summer; there are few better places to watch brownies than from the numerous salmon streams that flow into the nearby ocean. The sport-angling for cohoes and sockeye salmon is extremely good, too, if you do not mind meeting other fishermen in the streams — huge, furry ones.

Recently Roy Randall wrote me a letter about a new experience.

> I was out in the skiff the other morning and saw a bear lying on the beach alongside a dead sea lion. No way to know if the bear killed it or if it was washed ashore, dead. The wind was in my favor so I eased toward the beach, cut the engine and just drifted in. He was a big bear, 9 feet plus [estimated nose tip to tail tip], but

that sea lion may have doubled his weight. Big bulls will weigh a ton! After a minute or so the bear winded me, slowly got to its feet and walked out into the water up to its chest. He gave me one of those cold looks, mumbled something under his breath, and went back to his lion.

The bear took a bite into the back of the lion's neck and began to walk backward, trying to drag it. That lion's neck stretched like an old innertube and then darned if the carcass didn't begin to move. That bear dragged his prize up a steep bank over logs and all until it was hidden 50 yards back in the trees. I was very impressed.

THE GRIZZLY MASTER RACE

The brown bear is a most impressive beast, even if it may not scientifically deserve a special chapter in this book. Biologists and taxonomists have long agreed that the brown bears of coastal Alaska are only a larger race of the grizzly bear. In fact they *are* grizzly bears. But their edge-of-the-ocean environment, their diet, and perhaps some other yet-unknown factors have made brown bears slightly different from their kin, which roam the wilderness of interior Alaska. It has always seemed to me that brown bears are not only on average much larger than grizzlies, but they also have a somewhat different temperament.

The bears I will describe in this chapter are those that live only in the Alaskan coastal region (as well as on most of the coastal islands), no more than 50 miles inland from Baranof Island in southeastern Alaska, northwestward to Unimak Island, which lies beyond the tip of the Alaska Peninsula. The most famous and usually the largest of the brownies inhabit Kodiak Island, which has resulted in all brown bears sometimes being called Kodiaks. Brown bears have also been called coast bears, Peninsula brown bears, and even fish bears.

On average, Kodiak and polar bears are roughly the same size and are the largest carnivorous land mammals on earth. Of all land mammals, only elephants, rhinos, and hippos are bigger. The largest officially recorded bear was shot on Kodiak Island in 1952. The total length and width of its skull measured 30 $^{12}/_{16}$ inches. The largest known polar bear was slightly smaller at skull: 28 $^{12}/_{16}$ inches total length and width. But no one can, with authority, state that either the brown or the polar bear grows heavier. One polar bear specimen, now in the Carnegie Museum, was weighed in pieces after being shot. Even allowing for the loss of body fluids, its reported total weight was 1,728 pounds.

FISHING AND OTHER BEHAVIORS

Magnificent is an adjective too freely used to describe too many creatures; but in my mind, the brown bear truly lives up to the words. It is impossible to spend much time in brown-bear country and not be almost overwhelmed by the environment as well as its inhabitants. Kodiak, Afognak, and the Alaska Peninsula, where the great animals roam, are all places where the weather is capricious at best and downright foul a good part of the time, even during the brief Alaskan summer. Somehow that mist and penetrating cold enhance the feeling of genuine wilderness and magnificence.

The bears seem to begin moving as soon as a

downpour stops. One afternoon near the mouth of Chenik Creek, I had huddled for hours beneath a bank that had been undercut by a narrow stream, while trying to keep my camera and lenses dry. I shivered and, in time, even lost interest in the seething, skittering mass of humpback salmon packed into the stream just below. A red fox that seemed almost emaciated beneath its water-logged pelage, dragged a spawned-out salmon from a riffle out onto the gravel bank and began to eat it. The fox saw me and was not at all afraid. But I was too miserable to be excited.

Suddenly the picture changed. The pounding rain abated to a drizzle and stopped. As if on some signal, the fox darted away. And in its place, in the center of the creek, walked a brown bear. Salmon scattered ahead and all around it. The bear was splashing much too close for my own comfort.

When the bruin paid no more attention to me than the fox had, the instincts of a photographer won out over fear. I got ready to shoot. Some brown bears are expert fishermen, but this one rated among the most inept. The animal darted first this way and then another so quickly that I couldn't follow it through the long telephoto lens; the salmon always evaded it. I have often read that bears never actually bat salmon out of the water, and I agree that this is rarely the way bruins catch fish. But this bear finally succeeded in blasting a salmon out onto the bank with a wildly swinging forepaw. There the bear finally pounced upon the flopping salmon and ate it. I could actually focus on the pink eggs that were spilled from the salmon's body.

Brown bears have been described as courageous, intelligent, mean, crochety, morose, unpredictable, and even lazy. I suppose that at one time or another every bear could be any or all of these. But most of those Peggy and I have encountered are what might be described as "cool" or "laid-back." Through a high-magnification telephoto lens brown bears appear much less nervous than inland grizzlies, and more confident in their behavior. Admittedly this is an unscientific impression, though one that has been acquired over years of bear watching. I have never felt as uneasy near brown bears, despite their great size, as I do near inland grizzlies.

One morning, I sat on a bank overlooking Brooks River in what is now Katmai National Park and watched a bear catch and eat three salmon. Several gulls and a bald eagle sat surrounding it, waiting for scraps, as these birds commonly do on salmon-spawning streams. Most of the time, the bears pay little or no attention to the scavengers. But this particular brownie was clearly irritated. I could see the guard hairs rising on its shoulders.

At intervals the bear would make short passes at the birds, which always gave ground and even flew a short distance away. But the bruin was not mollified, and eventually it went charging crazily after the birds. Of course it never caught one. The birds only circled and landed next to the partially eaten fish.

It later occurred to me that those birds were deliberately annoying the bear until it left its catch unguarded. On a salmon stream where several bears are feeding at once on a multitude of spawning salmon, there are plenty of scraps scattered for all. But in the case described, only one bear was fishing, and few scraps were available for birds.

Frank Dufresne, chief officer of the U.S. Fish and Wildlife Service in Alaska before statehood, once described a similar incident to me. Gulls were crowding around a single bear feeding on salmon. When unable to drive them away, the bear transferred its frustration to the rotting tree stump on a nearby bank. With a single clout, the bruin sent a huge chunk of stump flying through the air. But even that wasn't enough to chase off the birds.

Browns, like inland grizzlies or blacks, endure the dark winter in underground hibernation. When a bruin emerges in spring, after months of fasting, it craves what could be called a spring tonic in skunk cabbage, hellebore, and the shoots of other green succulent plants. Brownies also have what is probably an instinctive craving for meat, which may be satisfied by digging out ground squirrels or hoary marmots until salmon begin their annual spawning runs into coastal rivers.

Some observers have credited brown bears with amazing skill in stalking and capturing deer and caribou, or even Dall sheep and moose. But brownies are not designed to be efficient pred-

Bears use body language and bluffing to establish rank when many bears concentrate in one place, as on the McNeil River. The strongest, largest males claim highest rank, young females without cubs the lowest. Different bears employ different techniques to catch salmon. But during the peak of the run, fish are plentiful enough for all bears to get enough to eat.

As red or sockeye salmon surge into clear coastal streams to spawn, brown bears gather to gorge on them, as here on Afognak Island.

Sockeyes are a silvery color when entering fresh water from the sea, but quickly change into their scarlet spawning color. The males also develop grotesque hooked jaws.

Spawning pink or humpback salmon practically choke certain coastal streams. Humpback males develop pointed, hooked jaws, but not the red color of sockeyes. Brown bears also relish the pinks.

◄ Early in the salmon season, bears will greedily eat the entire fish. Sated later on, they may strip out only the ripe eggs, and leave the rest for gulls and foxes to scavenge.

A female brings cubs on a fishing trip during the annual salmon-spawning run. The female must establish her "position" in the bear hierarchy, to ensure reasonably peaceful coexistence on the stream.

or more brownies met and responded to each other in some disruptive way. By recording which bear won and which bear lost each time, the scientist accumulated enough information to know that the McNeil salmon bears had a definite social hierarchy that worked fairly well.

Almost all bear encounters could be blamed on just four situations. Obviously the competition for a choice fishing spot was one problem. Violation of the distance or tolerance limit around one bear, which caused it to either run or attack, was another. A third reason was something called "redirected aggression," in which the loser in one encounter takes out its anger on a third bear. The fourth cause was the initial meeting between any two strange bruins. This often resulted in a physical contest that probably established their rank during the rest of the salmon run.

As in similar situations we have discussed, when bears (as well as other asocial animals) are cast together, the social hierarchy is based on size, sex, and reproductive condition. Bears in any group usually give ground to bears in higher-ranking groups. But these bears may remain very aggressive among themselves, since the ranking within the groups is not so well defined.

Large potent males are in a powerful group by themselves, and theirs is the top-ranking class. They stake out and defend the best fishing spots. At McNeil some dominant boars have "owned" the exact same fishing spots for several years. One animal would tolerate no competition for the last half of the 24 summers he was known to spend at the falls.

The second rank is composed of females with cubs; females without cubs are not in this group. Third from the top are sibling groups that travel together, often fish together, and throw their weight around as a single animal. Sometimes this succeeds more than other times. At the bottom of the McNeil hierarchy are unattached small males and females, with boars tending to rank higher, although size and age are also factors.

The age of a sow's cubs usually determines

In this typical scene on the McNeil River, an "inferior" female with cubs waits until a good fishing site is vacated by another bear. A troop of glaucous-winged gulls waits for scraps.

her place in her group. Those with yearlings or older cubs can afford to be much more aggressive than those with cubs only a few months old. For one thing the yearlings are not as fearful of life, and they imitate the mother's manner, seeming to stand up beside her in the face of trouble. On the other hand, a sow with fearful small cubs has her hands full just protecting them. But according to Stonorov, all sows with cubs are defensive to the point of being offensive. They are constantly threatening any other bears that come too near their offspring. More than once I have seen a McNeil sow lunge after a male, even a very large one, that wandered too near the cubs. It always seemed to me that in these instances, the male did little more than defend itself.

Many observers have noticed that the hierarchy of McNeil brown bears, or of brown bears gathered on any salmon stream, does not remain static. A dominant male brown may be less tolerant of a soon-to-be rival male than of a more inferior bear that is not a threat. Or a bruin with a stomach full of salmon may suddenly be more tolerant of a subordinate animal that has not eaten for some time.

COMMUNICATION

Sites such as McNeil Falls have been excellent laboratories for studying how bears communicate with one another, as they clearly do. The most noticeable communication signals are physical, such as either approaching or retreating slowly or at a run. Other messages include crouching, circling, lunging, backing up while facing a rival, standing motionless, or even sitting down. Low-ranking bears have even been observed lying down and approaching a larger animal on their stomachs.

Because of their very short tails and long hair, bears cannot use tails or torsos, as do other creatures, to send signals in "body language." That may explain why the head, neck, and mouth are used so much to convey a bruin's intentions. The

Three cubs on the McNeil River share, but not equally, the salmon provided by their mother.

position of the head is one of the most important indicators of a bear's mood.

For years, bear-country natives around the world have quickly interpreted a bear's mood by the position of its head. A Dene Indian living north of Yellowknife, Northwest Territory, who had spent a lifetime among barren-ground grizzlies, told me that the animals to watch were those that walked slowly with heads held down lower than the humps on the shoulders. A similar old Aleut belief is that a bear walking with head down is dejected, and is more likely to act aggressively—toward humans as well as other bears.

On the other hand, a bear of any species that walks with its head above the level of the shoulder (or shoulder hump with brown bears) is probably not looking for or expecting trouble. Brown bears, I think, walk with heads up more than inland grizzlies.

Brown bears use a whole range of face and mouth displays to intimidate one another. Sometimes simply staring at another bear is signal

enough to send it away. Opening and closing the mouth rapidly while salivating, or perhaps baring teeth or making a chomping noise, is usually very serious business. It means "get away from here now—or get ready to fight."

There is an almost human quality in bear signals and communications. One day, biologist Stonorov observed a large bear walk up behind a small one that was concentrating on catching a salmon. The smaller bear realized it was not alone when the big bear was only about 5 feet away. The bear turned around to look at the giant that was simply staring it down, and then fell over backward into the water.

Once during a four-day photographic session at McNeil Falls, I noticed through my telephoto lenses that some of the animals had wounds in their hides—some of these wounds quite large. I discussed this with Larry Aumiller, the Alaska Fish and Game Department biologist who has been stationed at the McNeil River for many summers. He said that the scars may have come from dominance fights or play-fighting right there on

This brown bear communicates with a bluffing body language as he approaches a desired fishing spot.

the McNeil, or from fighting over females during the May-June breeding season. Although Aumiller has witnessed hundreds of fights of varying intensity, and has seen blows inflicted that would have killed other animals, he does not know of a single encounter ending with a seriously crippled bear.

In a particularly fierce fight, a large boar gripped a 750-pound rival in its jaws and actually shook it. The exact weight of the victim is known because a few days later the bear was tranquilized and examined by biologists. A 20-square-inch piece of its hide had been torn away, and the flesh was bitten down to its ribs. But despite that damage, the wounded bear had been back on the river and fishing for salmon the day after the attack.

SOWS WITH CUBS

Even cubs seem to survive an occasional severe pummeling when an unrelated bear catches them beyond the protective custody of their mother. Until visiting a place such as McNeil, where bear meetings are so frequent, the tendency is to believe that cubs know only playful, carefree lives, guarded by devoted, avenging mothers. The latter part usually is true. Armed with great jaws, long teeth, and claws like forged steel, plus a hair-trigger temper, a female brown is an awesome deterrent to anyone or anything threatening her young ones. As long as her cubs remain underfoot, they are safe enough. Yet, studies of grizzly and brown cubs show that about 40 percent perish during their first year, and although the toll continues into the second year, it is lower. Thus, for reasons not entirely known, cubs face a good many dangers. I witnessed some of these dangers during filming on the McNeil River.

When the large brownie females waded out to fish, the cubs remained timidly along the bank, huddled together. Single cubs seemed the most frightened. Too often, the moment a strange bruin

Next pages: A female brown bear, fearful for her cubs, moves cautiously to a fishing spot.

Caution and patience in the bear hierarchy combine with the mother's fishing skill to bring the dinner.

approached, the young ones would dart into tall grass. Some would bawl for their mothers, which probably couldn't hear them above the din of McNeil Falls. In such situations it is easy for a dejected or low-level male bear to snatch and kill a cub.

Biologist Larry Aumiller reported that on a number of occasions, sows that arrived at the Falls with three cubs departed with only one or two. There is some evidence that brown-bear mothers have trouble counting and may not even realize that a cub is missing. One mother, however, had only two cubs when first seen in the area. A few days later she was trailed by four. Some cubs apparently cannot recognize their own mothers (or are not greatly concerned about them), and will attach themselves to any female that does not drive them away. Females do know their own cubs, but some seem willing to adopt and nurse— at least for a while—any lonely cub that persistently follows her. Larry Aumiller has noted that most families eventually sort themselves out.

Aumiller and his associate biologists have given many of the bears they meet at McNeil, year after year, human names such as Ladybird, Patches, Whitey, the Black Brothers, and Charlie Brown— who happened to be the top, or alpha, male at one time. At over 1,200 pounds, Charlie Brown rarely had to move a muscle. One day Ladybird was fishing in Charlie Brown's private spot while her triplet cubs huddled on the bank behind her, fearful, but hoping for a meal. That's when Charlie Brown arrived and walked sideways to his spot, trying to nudge the sow out of the way without having to hurt anybody. But Ladybird was an irritable and high-strung female. She roared and threatened with open mouth, her hair bristles standing on end. Charlie Brown ignored the theatrics and continued to push her out of the way. That was like flipping a switch. According to observers on the site, Ladybird let out a roar that drowned out the sound of the waterfall, and charged. But Charlie Brown was looking for it.

Intruders are urged to stay off good fishing turf with little regard for hurt feelings.

Once males are well-fed on salmon, they often play-fight for long hours along the McNeil River. We watched these two bears scuffling in the strong current for nearly an hour. Notice the open wound on the shoulder of one of the bears in the two photos at the bottom of the next page.

He swung around and caught her with a blow that lifted her quarter-ton body off the ground and onto her back. Then Charlie Brown turned to his fishing as if nothing had happened.

Life is not easy for sows with cubs. Although they need the nutrition more desperately than the already fatter males, there is rarely an equal opportunity to really concentrate on the fishing. Females are usually relegated to the second-best fishing spots. Sows must also be constantly concerned about cub safety.

One needn't spend much time on the McNeil River to realize that older females make better mothers than young ones. They are tougher disciplinarians, for one thing, and they are smarter. They are also higher in the hierarchy.

Whitey was a female that McNeil observers first noticed as a sub-adult because she was particularly inept at fishing. As in human anglers, fishing skill and techniques vary greatly among bears. Some bears wait patiently for a salmon to swim underfoot, while others try to trap fish in eddies, lunge at swimming fish, or even try swimming underwater for a catch. Of course, certain large bears take fish away from smaller ones. Whitey always expended plenty of energy, but little finesse, and so had a small effect on the salmon population.

One year Whitey arrived on the McNeil with her first brood. With a grunt that instructed the twin cubs to stay on shore, she plunged into the deep river and began searching for fish. Probably because she was an inexperienced and lenient mother, the cubs followed her out into the water. All brown bears are strong swimmers, including cubs; but the McNeil current was too great and Whitey's twins were swept downstream into an area already patrolled by several large boars. Any one of these bears could have grabbed and eaten the cubs. Whitey was preoccupied, and did not realize her cubs were missing until she heard their pitiful bawling becoming more and more faint in the distance. Suddenly she became frantic.

As fast as a young female brown bear can run (which is very fast), Whitey headed toward the vanishing sounds far downstream. She stopped

A bear with head lowered and gaze fixed in your direction is a bear that could be ready to test you.

only a few times to stand erect for a better view. Somehow she and the cubs got past the gauntlet of other bruins, and were reunited well below the bear's main fishing hole. The last the biologists saw of Whitey that day, she was suckling the cubs in the grassy glade beside that remarkable river.

PATCHES: THE GREAT BOAR

Perhaps the most interesting bear I met along the McNeil River was a great male known as Patches. In 1972, at the age of 16, he was described by another writer as a mountain of a brownie, "ancient, regal although somewhat ragged, with a balding behind." He was king of the west side of the river where he arrived, dependably, early every afternoon. His shuffling onto the scene was the signal for all other bears to clear out of the area. His fishing spot, if occupied, was quickly vacated.

Without working too hard at the game, but with bewildering speed and agility for such an awesome beast, Patches caught one salmon after another. One observer reported that he caught as many as 20 salmon averaging 6 pounds apiece without missing. Hungrier in the beginning, he ate entire fish before discarding males and eating only females. When nearly full, Patches gorged only on ripe, pink eggs, allowing the glaucous winged gulls and ravens to consume the rest. Incidentally, Patches may not have been a prodigious eater in relation to his bulk. Individual bears have often taken more than 20 salmon a day, and there is one McNeil record of a single bear catching 69 salmon during one long summer's daylight.

In 1979, at 23 years old, Patches was still premier bear on his side of the river, but his grip was slipping. Not all bears always or immediately gave him his right of way. More than a swish of the head or a stare was sometimes necessary to assure his space around his fishing hole. I last saw Patches in late July, 1980, and he was still coming every afternoon to that same favorite spot. He was then 24 and looked it. He walked very slowly and after an hour of fishing and eating, would fall asleep right on his station, much as an old man might after a heavy Sunday dinner.

All during the nap, other bears fished nearby, much closer than they would ever have dared in the past. Patches was reaching the end of his reign. Yet many of the bears on the McNeil River were his progeny, including the one that would finally drive him away.

PROTECTING MAN AND BEAR

I have described the bears and their activities along the McNeil in great detail because the area is among the finest wildlife spectacles and wildlife study laboratories on earth. There is no better proof anywhere that bears and humans can stand side by side, without harm to either, if definite, sensible rules are observed.

In this sanctuary, only ten humans at ony one time, each selected by lottery, camp in just one restricted area. There are no formal accommodations whatsoever. You transport everything you need for any visit by charter seaplane. People follow a single path for 1½ miles from the designated campsite to a single viewing site overlooking McNeil Falls. All other real estate belongs to the bears.

In Larry Aumiller's words, "except for an occasional sidelong glance, the bears seemingly ignore and accept the human interlopers." Since 1973, when the current strict regulations were first enforced, there has not been a single bear-man incident, which is a tribute to the administrators as well as to the bruins.

It is well worth reviewing the history of the McNeil area because it reveals much about bear behavior. In 1955, the then-territorial Alaskan government closed most of the McNeil River watershed to hunting to protect its unusual concentration of brown bears. Twelve years later the Alaskan state legislature designated 85,000 critical acres as a state game sanctuary. But before 1973 there were no regulations governing visitors or their activities in the sanctuary. Anyone could camp anywhere, even amid bear concentrations. People came in ever greater numbers, and accumulating garbage became a problem. One of the first wildlife wardens on the scene told me that human behavior was much more unpredictable than that of the bears. It soon became apparent that the unlimited number of visitors and

This large male brown eats a salmon right where he caught it. Others carry the catch onto shore, safely away from other bears.

Fishing skills vary widely among bears. Cubs learn from their mothers. Some learn well.

their strange antics were discouraging bears from feeding at the falls. The problem had become so serious that between 1970 and 1972 only half as many bears were appearing during the annual salmon runs. It was time to initiate the restrictions in force today.

As it turned out, few plans have ever worked as well. Now it is not at all unusual to see 30 different bears at McNeil Falls in a single day. Most of these might be on-site at one time. Summed up, Alaska's system of consistent, regulated, non-aggressive human presence has succeeded in creating a wildlife-watching opportunity unmatched in the world.

But the McNeil River safety record should in no way be misconstrued. Traveling in bear country anytime, anywhere, calls for extreme caution. Too many Alaskans have not lived to regret their carelessness. Jay Reeves, 38, an amateur but experienced wildlife photographer, was unfortunately among them. His case is typical.

Early on an August afternoon, he pitched his one-man tent on the bank of Frosty Creek, about 7 miles from Cold Bay on the Izembek National Wildlife Refuge. This is excellent brown-bear range, located at the western tip of the Alaska Peninsula. Only a year earlier another man, Pat Wren, had disappeared during a hike in the same area. Some thought Wren had drowned, but others felt he had been killed by a bear. The mystery remains unsolved.

The day after Reeves had established his camp, a federal biologist in a helicopter spotted Reeves' tent and, about ½ mile away, Reeves' headless, partly devoured body. Minutes after the gruesome discovery, John Sarvis arrived and found and shot the 8½-foot male brown bear that had killed Reeves. Its stomach contained human flesh, bones, and part of a pack of cigarettes.

In Cold Bay, magistrate Karl Heiker rendered a verdict of accidental death. Since Reeves was unarmed, there was no evidence that the attack was provoked. But Reeves had made at least one terrible mistake. He had pitched his tent very near

Dozens of brown bears are killed annually in defense of life and property. It is conjectural how many of these kills are made when a bear simply rises to get a better view of an intruder.

a trail frequently used by bears in search of spawning salmon, and where another man had vanished. Because the wind velocity had reached gusts of 60 knots during that night, investigators believe that the noisy flapping of Reeves' tent may have attracted the five-year-old bruin to the spot. It probably attacked the man while he was sleeping and dragged him away, because his boots were found at the campsite.

Ed Bailey, a U.S. Fish and Wildlife Service biologist who was once stationed at Izembek and has long lived among brown bears, could only describe the Reeves incident as bizarre. Although there have been incidents in that part of Alaska of brown bears devouring people who died of other causes, Bailey knew of no other incidents in which brownies killed and ate the victims. Nor did hunger seem to be the reason for the attack, because there were ample supplies of berries and fish on the refuge at the time. Tests of the bear's head for rabies proved negative.

Too many brown bears are shot every year in what might be termed defense of life, or possible defense of life. The line between the two is hazy at best. The endless tales about the great size and ferocity of the species have probably caused some triggers to be pulled before it was necessary. But in October 1977, Ken McConnell, Don Card, and Floyd Poage, hunting black bears where the Killey River flows into Alaska's Kenai River, were confronted with a brown bear that was both huge and fearsome.

The three men had traveled by boat to the river's confluence where they planned to separate and hunt in different directions. But almost immediately McConnell met a large bear in dense cover. When it stood on its hind legs, the hunter began walking backward toward his friends. And when the bear seemed to be trying to cut him off he started to shout. Still the animal kept coming.

The shouting alerted Poage and Card, who came running. When they saw the bear, for which the hunting season was closed, all screamed at the top of their lungs to turn it away. But the bear

As long as people abide by regulations regarding brown bears, photographers will continue to have opportunities to capture these magnificent creatures on film.

In Alaska, regulations that keep man from intruding too much in brown-bear territory have succeeded in providing excellent bear-watching opportunities.

continued toward the men, making grunting and barking sounds, as one recalls. When it was only 30 feet away, all fired and killed the animal. As the law required, the hunters immediately notified the Department of Fish and Game.

By coincidence, the investigating officer was Al Thompson who himself had been mauled by a brown bear on the Funny River a few years before. Because the animal was shot out of season in defense of life, Thompson had to confiscate the hide and skull. The hide squared out at 9½ feet and the skull, which measured 29 inches (combined length and width), can be seen today in the Homer Museum. It is the largest brown-bear skull (by 1 inch) ever taken on the Kenai Peninsula. It is also close to the largest skull of all which was taken on Kodiak Island.

This Kenai bear was one of 37 browns or grizzlies killed in defense of life or property in Alaska in 1977 by other than sport or trophy hunters. The average number of such reported kills varies annually from 35 to 45. That number does not include many that go unreported for various reasons. One of the kills reported in 1977 was of a huge brown struck by a speeding automobile near Eagle River.

Investigator Thompson could find no reason why the bear behaved aggressively toward the Kenai hunters. It probably was not guarding a food cache. But it was very old (about 22 years), and Alaska bear specialist Lee Miller speculated that it did not have much longer to live anyway. The canine teeth were either broken off or worn down to the gums. But what baffled Miller more than the bruin's behavior was the fact that it was able to live so long, apparently without getting into other trouble near a comparatively populated area. Brown bears are normally wilderness creatures.

Like all bears, every brown is different. Most live their lives free of conflict with humans. Says Lee Miller: "Check out a dozen different brown bears dispatched in defense of life and you will probably find a dozen different reasons why they behaved as they did."

CHAPTER 4
POLAR BEARS

The revered and often quoted naturalist Ernest Thompson Seton wrote in 1909: "For centuries, it has been the custom of Arctic travelers to kill all Polar Bears they could. It did not matter whether the travellers needed the carcasses or not. In recent years, this senseless slaughter increased, since more travellers went north, and deadlier weapons were carried. One Arctic explorer told me that he personally had killed 200 Polar Bears, and secured but few of them.

"The Canadian Government determined to stop this wicked destruction, yet sought for a good reason to offer the public. The naturalists supplied it: Every Polar Bear is followed all winter by a retinue of White Foxes, who live on the scraps of his table. Without him, they would die. Therefore, the Polar Bear is conserving a valuable fur supply. So the law was passed; today, the Polar Bear is protected as a high-class game animal."

Today the polar bear—known also as the ice bear, or Arctic or great white bear, *Thalarctos maritimus*—is fairly well protected all around the world. It is a living treasure that belongs to no one nation, wandering about the ice of the northern hemisphere and making sojourns onto the lands of Alaska, Canada, Norway, Greenland, and the Soviet Union. Although the bear's seemingly playful antics observed in zoos make it familiar to almost everyone, it remains an enigmatic and mysterious resident of our planet, which relatively few people have ever seen in the wild.

International agreements are now saving the polar bear from extinction.

PHYSIQUE

No other large land mammal is as well adapted to life in such a cold, white environment. The polar bear survives by being a successful predator of other large carnivores, namely Arctic species of seals. As naturalist Seton described it, an ice bear captured a 100-pound seal in the water and then climbed out onto an ice floe with the prey in its teeth "as easily as a mink coming ashore with a trout." Other Arctic observers have verified this portrayal of the strength, agility, and swimming ability of one of the largest meat eaters living on land. Only the Alaskan brown bear rivals it in size. The massive forepaws of a polar bear may be larger than a dinner plate, and larger than the hindpaws. They have powerfully muscled, elongated, agile bodies. With partially webbed toes and long, powerful claws, the polar bear is able to swim rapidly, dig easily in snow or ice, and kill a 500-pound bearded seal with ease.

White bears probably evolved from the brown forest bears relatively recently, about 250,000 years ago. As they emerged from forests to feed on seals, they became more and more at home on ice. They have been clocked from a hovering helicopter running over the ice pack at 25 miles per hour. There are reports of bears swimming as far as 300 miles between floes. Thick, oily fur suspends the bruins in frigid water and enables them to float or swim for hours at a time. The color of the hair isn't really white. In fact polar bear hair is colorless. Some scientists believe that ultraviolet light funnels through the hair to the bruin's body, making each animal an efficient, hairy solar collector. A polar bear's white appearance results when the individual hairs, with hollow interiors, scatter light in the same way as ice and snow, which also contain no white pigment.

Nature has also equipped polar bears with built-in "sunglasses" to prevent snowblindness, which would be deadly to them. The eyes are protected from glare by a special lid, which acts as a polarizer. Still, a polar bear's eyesight is not as keen

This huge, splendid female was filmed near Cape Merry, Manitoba, near the mouth of the Churchill River. The polar bear is one of the two largest land carnivores surviving today. Only coastal brown bears of Alaska may reach comparable size.

Polar bears are extremely strong swimmers, able to travel great distances between ice floes in bitter cold.

as its superb sense of smell that enables it to scent seal blubber from as far as 20 miles away on the uncontaminated polar air.

BEARS AS HUNTERS

Mature females may weigh 500 pounds and mature boars more than twice that. Creatures of such huge size must travel far in a never-ending hunt for enough calories to survive. Despite its great bulk, a polar bear can lower itself backward into the sea, making little more than a ripple. Then it can swim underwater, or on the surface with only its nose showing, and suddenly lunge out of the water to capture a seal on the ice.

There is absolutely nothing clumsy or hesitant about the movements of a polar bear, which have been described as almost snakelike, when stalking a seal that is resting on the ice. Crouching low to the ice, the bear eases or even slides forward almost imperceptibly on its belly. Despite its speed afoot, its ability to leap 6-foot hurdles, and to scale vertical ice cliffs, a bear is extremely patient when closing in on a meal. It stops moving whenever a wary seal wakes up from a nap, and then remains motionless until its prey dozes

again. Eskimos have reported that, when stalking, a polar bear covers its black nose (which is all that does not blend into the white background) with a foreleg.

Once close enough to the target, the stalker springs into running position and races forward in a blur of motion. If the victim is small it is killed instantly. Subduing a large seal may leave blood and the signs of vicious struggle over an acre or more of ground. My friend Sam Miller, who studied bears for many years in the Canadian Arctic, told me that the site of a carmine-colored recent seal kill might be one of the few distinguishable marks on a vast all-white landscape that extends in all directions to the horizons.

Although a polar bear must be energetic and tireless in its pursuit of food, it is the catlike patience that makes it successful on most hunts. In fact, most of an ice bear's behavior as well as its anatomy is adapted specifically to hunting seals—which are either bearded or ringed, depending on the location. Even the bear's own long neck (more like a black bear's neck than a grizzly's) resembles the smooth profile of a seal. In this case both predator and prey have keen senses and are intelligent. But it is the seal that

In profile, a polar bear has a long neck and resembles a black bear more than a grizzly or brown bear. Its coat is a pale cream color, rather than pure white.

ties the polar bear to the sea and to hunting over the icy wilderness for its primary food.

Seals evolved long ago from carnivorous land mammals. Although fish-like in form, and subsisting largely on fishes and shrimp, they must rise to the surface every few minutes to breathe. They must also emerge from the water to give birth and to rest occasionally. This vulnerability is what makes them prey to the ice bear. When there is an absence of open water during the long circumpolar winters, seals must breathe through small blowholes, which they keep open by frequently gnawing on the accumulated ice. They thereby make it possible for bears to survive. It is no coincidence that polar bears (except denning

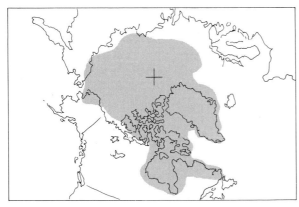

The polar bear's circumpolar range varies with the seasons. With the melting of polar ice, the bears retreat to land.

pregnant females) are found almost everywhere the seal abounds, and vice versa.

DISTRIBUTION FACTORS

A polar bear's seasonal activities and meanderings are dictated by the extent and distribution of polar ice. Each winter, the vast polar ice is nearly surrounded by hundreds of miles of so-called pack ice. This is a hazardous terrain formed of great blocks and slabs of ice jammed, piled, and crushed into a shifting mass by winter storms, intense cold, and Arctic sea currents. Seals and other marine mammals are attracted to the edge of this pack ice, as well as to the long, open channels or "leads" formed in the pack by tides and currents. Polar bears are, in turn, attracted to these prey species.

Beginning in early spring, even the resistant inshore ice begins to break up, creating an ideal situation for seals and bruins. As the area of pack ice gradually dwindles with the arrival of the Arctic summer, most bears apparently move onto more solid footing. Or they may make landfalls on distant Arctic shores or on certain islands far from human settlement. During this summer period, some bears may be carried great distances by ice floes drifting on ocean currents. Much scientific work has been done on polar bears in recent years, but we still do not fully understand their movements throughout the year.

OBSERVED BY BOAT

I have been lucky enough to see polar bears on several occasions, and even to spend many cold and windy days filming them. But only on two occasions have I seen the animals far out on the polar ice pack.

Once while cruising aboard the *Lindblad Explorer*, a ship equipped with a double hull for ice-breaking and polar navigation, we came upon a vast area of large floes and broken ice north of

As October blends into November, more and more polar bears migrate from summer resting areas inland toward the edge of Hudson Bay. There they await freeze-up along a rocky or grassy shoreline strewn with icebergs.

Akpatok Island, in the Canadian sub-Arctic. This bleak, uninhabited landfall lies north of Hudson Bay and is a known *hauling out island*, that is, an island where the bears come on shore. We were slowly breaking our way through the loose ice when we spotted a female with two half-grown cubs. At first the three did not seem unduly afraid, even with the loud crunching of ice around the bow as we motored ahead. In fact, the female paused to study the giant red-hulled vessel until we were only 50 yards or so away. Then all three turned and ran, alternately swimming from one ice floe to another until they were out of sight. It was a fine demonstration of the ease and confidence with which polar bears can travel over that half-frozen environment.

Several days later we spotted a single white bear asleep on an iceberg. Apparently it was slumbering very soundly, because we drifted to within about 10 yards before it stood erect and stretched. Only when the boat was about to bump the large berg did the bear hurry away out of sight beyond irregular ice ridges. Since then I've often pondered the bear's lack of concern about the sudden appearance of an ocean-going vessel looming near and above it.

MATING

Polar-bear mating takes place on the disintegrating pack ice during April and May when daylight hours are lengthening. Mating may occur as late as the end of June when the sun virtually never sets in the Far North. Among many of the world's so-called big-game species in which the male is much larger than the female, the male acquires a harem during the annual breeding season. But that is not true of polar or any other North American bears. A male may mate with any number of females during a summer or a lifetime, and a female may copulate with many males; but this probably depends on bear density, and on how widely the animals wander in search of mates.

According to Eskimos and biologists, a female coming into estrus may begin to wander at a faster pace, stopping often to urinate, thereby marking her trail. If there are males in the vicinity, they will soon pick up the scent and follow the trail. Sam Miller tells of seeing lone male polar bears many miles apart, but all walking briskly in their characteristic stride toward a single female objective. Fierce fights can occur whenever they converge. While these encounters are seldom fatal, deaths are not unknown.

I have never seen polar boars in serious combat. But I have often watched and photographed male ice bears scuffling and play-fighting, which may just be practice for the main event. The boars' clubbing action, often done while standing on hind feet, is invariably sudden and dramatic enough to give some idea of the real thing.

Like all bruins worldwide, the male polar bear has a *baculum*, which is a penis bone. It resembles an ivory hammer handle and is much prized by Eskimos, especially by the man who may have killed the bear. Occasionally a bear is killed and found to have a fractured baculum, which has led to native legends about violent mating rituals. But at least among specimens in captivity, that is not the case. The only violence during breeding involves the rival males.

After mating, boars and sows may never meet again. Through a process of delayed implantation, the fertilized egg (or eggs) carried by the female does not begin to develop until about September. By late fall, the female will have acquired a solid blubber layer that will later serve as a food reserve.

SOLITARY OR GREGARIOUS?

Polar bears have long been known as loners, or as antisocial in behavior. But more and more we are learning that this is not necessarily true. If polar bears seem to be solitary nomads, it is simply that successful seal hunting requires keeping a certain distance apart. A single cautious hunter in an area will always be less evident to the prey than will two or more hunters. In fact, the more bears there are hunting over an expanse of ice, the less likely many of them will capture

We photographed this bear from a boat while cruising the gray waters of Canada's Northwest Passage.

Photo next page: The bear didn't seem frightened by our very close approach by boat.

enough meat to survive.

But once the busy hunting season ends and melting ice drives polar bears out onto firm ground, they usually tolerate each other's company and at times may even enjoy it. More than once on the barrens around Churchill, Manitoba—where many bears congregate every fall until Hudson Bay freezes over—I have seen small groups getting along well, or at least tolerating one another.

For several consecutive days I watched three males of medium size play-fighting together, strolling in single file along the shallow shoreline, and occasionally sleeping on frozen potholes during rare sunny days. It is possible the three were siblings, but the association is noteworthy nonetheless. They could have separated, but elected not to do so. On other occasions I have seen as many as a dozen bears around Cape Churchill in autumn, using the same general area without conflict. Several bears have often been observed feeding together peacefully on the beached carcasses of beluga whales.

Generally, though, the largest bears in a vicinity are dominant. Lesser bears give the larger boars a wide berth. Females with cubs also try to keep plenty of distance between themselves and males. On two occasions, however, I've seen females leave their cubs just long enough to make swift, angry charges toward males that came too near.

Incidentally, in time one can usually distinguish males from females, even at a distance. Males are rangier in general appearance, and walk more directly toward a destination with much more confidence in their stride. They also tend to have longer, leaner faces that appear darker around the muzzle. Older males may appear even more yellow or cream-colored than white. The area around the head may be scarred from fighting, and darker hairs grow around the scars. Biologists who have worked with polar bears for a long time can even tell individuals apart. The body language of a bear also reveals much about its age, sex, and status in the bear community.

Some old Eskimos believe females are more skillful seal hunters than most males. One veteran in Coral Harbor told me that he saw large males drive females away from seals the females had just captured. He said he had found evidence of this on many occasions. On the other hand, there are a few reports of passing bears sharing a seal kill before drifting apart again.

DENNING AND BIRTHING

Unlike other bears, polar-bear males do not hibernate; instead, they spend the winter in a never-ending seal hunt. Some of this pursuit continues during the dark of night because, for a period, there is little daylight during the polar winter. But females, about to produce cubs eight months after springtime mating, will move onto a remote shore to find or build a maternity den in October or November. Initially a maternity den may be only a shallow depression in a ridge or esker. But the den is usually located so that in time it will be completely covered by drifting snow. During the northern Canadian winter, prior to the birth of the cubs, the females shape out a special oval chamber under the snowdrift. Biologists have entered and examined a number of these bear dens and found chambers measuring up to 20 feet long, by 5 feet in height and width. Access was by an entrance tunnel that averaged 6 feet long and about 2 feet in diameter, with a raised sill. A polar bear den is not unlike an Eskimo igloo.

When at last she enters the den to be snowed in, the female is not only pregnant but also very fat. Because the covering snow is good insulation, the denning bear's body heat alone will maintain a temperature of as high as 40° F inside, while outside the mercury is far below freezing. The greater the depth of accumulated snow drift, the warmer it remains inside. A denning sow is torpid with a lowered body temperature and reduced respiratory rate to conserve energy. But Sam Miller is one of several investigating biologists who discovered that this is far from a complete state of hibernation. A "sleeping" polar bear awakens easily, and with irritation.

In Canada, the young are born during December or January, the coldest and darkest period of the year. The mother may not even be aware of the birth. When born, the cubs are in a very early stage of development; they are born blind, helpless, and smaller than an adult prairie dog. Three

These medium-size male bears are play-fighting on a frozen pond near Churchill, Manitoba. Play-fighting establishes rank and conditions the animals for hunting seals over frozen Arctic oceans in winter. (Photo series continues on next page.)

or four more months will pass before they first glimpse daylight. Until March or April the sow sustains from one to four cubs (though usually two or three) by nursing. The milk, which has a nutty taste, is extremely rich, thick, and nourishing. In March or April the family finally leaves the den, never to see it again.

March or April is the ideal time for a now-gaunt female to head her cubs out onto the ice because that is when seal pups are born. Now the female spends all her time and energy searching and sniffing out the snow and ice dens where the pups have been hidden by parents. Hunting, fortunately, is never easier for polar bears. The bear family hunts together until the second autumn of the yearlings, at which time 1½-year-old young are often deserted. Yet some families may actually remain intact for 2½ years. One fall in Manitoba, Peggy and I spent several days photographing a female with triplet yearlings on the Hudson Bay shores near Churchill. The next year we found the four still together in virtually the same place at the same time. By then each cub was two-thirds the size of its mother.

Curiously, most polar bear denning sites are concentrated in about 18 definite areas over their circumpolar range, rather than simply scattered evenly. One well-known area is on Wrangell Island north of eastern Siberia. Another, one of the world's largest, was not really discovered until 1969. Its center is about 50 miles south of the mouth of the Churchill River, and north of the Nelson River, in northeastern Manitoba, in the Broad River-Owl River drainages. Every winter there are an estimated 50 maternity dens in this region. Still another denning place is located just south of the Nelson River, with some other sites not far away near Cape Henrietta Maria on James Bay. Perhaps some other polar bear denning areas are yet undiscovered.

WINTER AND SUMMER DEN SITES

It may seem mysterious that so many denning white bears and denning sites in Manitoba could have remained unknown for so long. The reason is apparent when you see the nearly impassable, roadless terrain. Mostly it is wet and boggy with

(Play-fighting continued)

Next page: Peggy and I photographed these bears during a November dusk walking directly toward the shore of Hudson Bay, as if guided by radar, to join other bruins waiting there. Three days later, the Bay had suddenly frozen solid and no bears could be found in sight.

only a few small streams draining eastward toward Hudson Bay. In summer the area is a nightmare of buzzing, biting flies. Even a powerful man can walk only a few miles a day across the spongy land on foot. There has never been much reason for anyone to explore here. The low-lying muskeg, punctuated with stunted black spruce and tamarack, is underlain by deep layers of peat. The area is even difficult to reach by water because the shallow, soft, tidal flats extend out into Hudson Bay as far as 6 miles in places.

Many polar bears also use this Manitoba-northern Ontario denning area in summer, the period when Hudson Bay and Arctic waters to the north are ice-free. This same geography that keeps maternity dens warmer in winter also offers cool retreats during the frequent hot days of summer. The bruins simply dig deep pits beneath hammocks and low ridges until they reach permafrost, where it is possible to rest in cool peace. As summer progresses and the exposed permafrost melts, it often becomes necessary to dig deeper and deeper. That probably explains the reason for some extremely deep bear dens researchers have found, which may have been in use for centuries. Some of the underground sanctuaries may also be occupied during the hot months by more than one animal at a time.

THE DAYS OF SUMMER

The location of these summer dens is handy for another reason besides the permafrost coolant. Some food, both vegetable and animal, exists along the Hudson Bay coast. (Polar bears are not 100 percent carnivores. They do eat grasses and berries when on land.) This summertime denning inland may be a throwback to the time when polar bears were evolving from forest creatures.

By the time the Arctic tundra begins to bloom every spring, most polar bears turn from vagabonding over frozen seas onto either familiar or handy landfalls. Probably most return to the approximate vicinity—if not the exact place—

A mother bear with cubs travels and watches apprehensively for the approach of other larger bears. Her life is far from trouble-free because males may kill and eat unprotected cubs.

A female polar bear with two nearly full-grown (2½-year-old) cubs relaxes in late summer in northeastern Manitoba. This is the last summer the family will spend together. When Hudson Bay freezes, the cubs will have to forage over ice for themselves.

where they were born. A Siberian bear, for instance, will spend the summer on a lonely Siberian island. Greenland bears make their way back to familiar scenes on that big island. Several hundred Hudson Bay bruins return to the area south of Churchill.

When out on the winter ice, a bear blends perfectly into its surroundings. But in summer every animal is conspicuous against the green or brown landscape where it may occasionally go hunting between periods of indolence. The bears adapt easily to the change of diet from seal to blueberries and kelp. For a time it is fairly easy to rob the flightless chicks from the nests of waterfowl and shorebirds. Now and then a dead beluga whale may wash up onto a beach at high tide. The summer fare may not be as nutritious as raw seal meat, but it suffices for a few months, and the change may even be necessary to the species' overall health.

THE AUTUMN WAIT AT CHURCHILL

As lazy summer blends into autumn, the bears spend proportionately less time napping as they move nearer to the shoreline, which they prowl, awaiting freeze-up and the chance to get back on the ice. Only the pregnant females remain on shore and begin the search for maternity den sites.

This shifting toward the shoreline results in unusual concentrations of polar bears, as occurs

This family near Churchill, Manitoba, spends a summer day as though posing for a cartoonist.

annually in the vicinity of Churchill and the mouth of the Churchill River. As many as 300 have been counted within the general area in a single fall season. We have seen as many as 30 bears during a mid-November day there; in fall it is the best place on earth for anyone to see, often at close range, these magnificent wild beasts.

The bear concentration around Churchill has also caused its share of problems and incidents, as I will discuss later.

Social behavior regulates which places individual bears occupy while they wait for solid ice to form. Adult males claim the choice spots right at the water's edge. Large females with cubs or yearlings are stationed slightly inland. Cubless females and young males are pushed still farther inland. Although some individuals have been spotted as far as 100 miles inland, most gather within a few miles of the shore from October onward. Final freeze-up in the Churchill area usually occurs in mid-November. Almost overnight, a landscape that contained many bears is suddenly empty of the conspicuous white animals.

THE TOLL OF FUR HUNTING

For the centuries man has explored in the Arctic, it has been customary to kill any polar bear encountered. As long as the hunters were Eskimos with primitive weapons, the toll wasn't too great on either side. They hunted with dogs, which hazed the bears, and the killing was done at close range with crude, homemade weapons. But firearms and even whalers' harpoons began to take an ever greater toll. But that was only the beginning.

Only a few centuries ago, polar bears were sometimes seen as far south as northern Japan. Jacques Cartier, the 16-century French explorer, reported seeing a bruin as big as a cow and "as white as a swan" on Funk Island, Newfoundland, which was then also the home of the great auk, now extinct. There were even scattered reports of seeing "white" bears near the mouth of the St. Lawrence River in the early 1700s. Because polar bear pelts had become status symbols in Europe during the 19th century, the sealers and whalers

Having moved from its inland summer retreat, this bear frequents the shore in anticipation of the freeze-up.

who sailed the polar regions made a special attempt to obtain them. But sport hunting by small aircraft and motor vessels in the 20th century is what gravely threatened the species. Thousands were being killed every year. It was only the extreme inaccessibility of their environment that has assured survival to this day. The total number left on earth was recently estimated at between 10,000 and 15,000 or so.

Polar bears are now probably as secure as might be expected at a time when the world's wild places are so rapidly being destroyed. In an unusual spirit of cooperation, the five countries where the species exists agreed to a moratorium on hunting, and none too soon; in the early 1980s, prime "rugs" sold for as high as $10,000, with Japan a principal purchaser. There is still incentive to poach. Some subsistence hunting by native peoples is permitted in Canada, though this is not likely to be damaging. But future mass extraction of petroleum or other minerals in Arctic regions where seals and bears thrive could be disastrous.

The United States, Norway, Canada, and the Soviet Union have engaged in some polar-bear study. One result has been to dispel an old belief that polar bears are aimless travelers, marching over the ice from continent to continent. Eskimos referred to the ice bear as *pihoqahiaq*, which roughly translates into "always wandering one." Biologists now know that the total population is made up of several distinct populations living within specific boundaries. There is that Hudson Bay population, for instance, which lives part of the year ashore in Manitoba.

POLAR BEAR LORE

It is impossible to travel far among Arctic villages and not hear an endless number of polar bear stories, some not unlike the tales of abominable snowmen or the Loch Ness monster. A few older Eskimos from Coral Harbor to Cape Dorset talk about Kokogiak, a legendary monster of the jagged ice floes, which some citizens claim to have seen. It is a white bruin with ten legs and four or five times as big as a polar bear.

Some bears restlessly patrol the shore of Hudson Bay waiting for the final freeze-up. After that, they disappear into the dark water. The survivors of winter return just before the spring breakup.

Another story Eskimos like to tell concerns one of the Dew Line early-warning stations the United States built across the Arctic just after World War II. One night the men at one station were baffled to see the lights go out on the nearby runway one after another. Since nothing was wrong with the generator, they investigated outside and found tracks of a large female polar bear with a cub. The playful cub had gone up and down the runway, smashing the lights.

The men grabbed rifles and went looking for the bears with only the headlights of their jeep to light the way. Although they spent several hours searching the vicinity of the station, they were lucky never to have caught up with the bears. According to the Eskimo telling the story, the extreme cold had congealed the oil in the rifles, making them inoperative.

There is something eerie about finding yourself out on a vast tundra, without a shelter or a climbable tree in sight, and suddenly having a polar bear materialize on the scene. That has happened to me twice.

One October Peggy, Bob Bridge, and I were hunting snow geese on the Cape Tatnam Wildlife Management Area, Manitoba. We had flown by light plane into a rough landing strip that, from the air, seemed no bigger than a postage stamp beside the cluster of wooden shacks that would be our camp. The tundra all around was full of migrating waterfowl getting ready to go southward. Next morning in the pre-dawn darkness, we hiked out a mile or so from camp and quickly made hasty shooting blinds from Arctic willows cut on the spot. Geese began flying as soon as it was light enough to shoot, and we dropped three from the first flight. One fell a hundred yards away, where the snow-white plumage was easy to spot.

"But what is that other white thing out there?" Peggy asked.

Looking through his binocular, Bob answered, "It's the head of a polar bear." The animal had been watching us all the while.

We kept on shooting that morning, but with a very uneasy feeling. The bear did not come any closer, or even move from its position. But at intervals it sat upright for a better look at us. When we headed back for camp, we watched over our shoulders all the way. I didn't even bother to collect the one snow goose that had fallen far away. Next morning, we waited until after daybreak before leaving camp, not wanting to stumble on a bear in the dark. We never did see that bear again.

On another occasion we were floating down the North Knife River in extreme northeastern Manitoba, and at noon pulled up onto a bare river bar to broil several grayling we had caught en-route. Again we were on a treeless landscape, but never gave that fact a thought. Suddenly, a white bear was standing on the opposite bank, swinging its head with nose held high as if trying to sniff more information about us from the air.

"Let's take those paddles and get that canoe in the water," I said softly, being careful to make no sudden moves.

Seemingly uncertain, the bear made a step toward the water, but then seemed to change its mind. It turned away and vanished in the stunted willows. But we immediately left the spot, and didn't stop paddling for several miles. We broiled our fish in another spot far downstream.

How big do polar bears grow? The heaviest polar bear we could locate on record was a 1,450 pound Canadian male accurately weighed by Dr. Charles Jonkel in 1971. In truth, very few 1,000-pounders exist in the world, despite all claims. During the last decade or two, countless bears have been live-captured and weighed in the Churchill area of Manitoba. But as late as 1983, the heaviest bear on record there was a male that weighed just under 900 pounds. The average female is less than half the weight of the average male. It is among the wonders of nature that a creature weighing only a half pound at birth can eventually reach such immense size during a life spent mostly on polar pack-ice.

The fact that any animal can find food out on the vast expanse of polar ice may seem impossible. But forests of kelp grow unseen beneath the ice, and the undersea ecosystem includes fish, starfish, abundant shrimp, anemones, as well as many mollusks, crustaceans, and sea worms. Ringed seals, which are almost as widespread in range as the pack ice itself, feed on all of these and, in turn, are fed on by polar bears. Ringed seals are small members of the pinniped family, rarely exceeding 200 pounds. But polar bears also prey on bearded seals as a second source of food. Bearded seals can weigh up to 1,000 pounds.

Not many humans ever have the opportunity to watch polar bears hunting and observe their techniques. Ian Stirling of the Canadian Wildlife Service is one of a few. For several years, he spent the spring and summer on a high cliff overlooking a bay of Devon Island in the Canadian high Arctic. It was a splendid and safe vantage point for watching the bruins capture seals far below. Most of the bears preferred patient still-hunting beside breathing holes, seizing the seal when it surfaced to replenish its air supply. Others stalked either by water or overland, whichever seemed best. Often a bear would resort to a very complicated stalk to reach its quarry, swimming part of the way, then creeping and crawling. Some of the bears seemed to be better hunters than others. A few even seemed indifferent to hunting at the time, which may have resulted from being too well fed.

A hungry polar bear gulps down a seal, including many of the bones and the flippers. But other bears play with captured seals, much as a cat torments a mouse. The typical bruin eats the skin and blubber first. In times of plenty when the hunting is easy, a bear may eat only the skin and blubber. Stirling noted that if a female with cubs killed the seal, virtually nothing of the carcass ever remained. Scraps from any seal kill are soon found by Arctic foxes, ravens, gulls.

There are scattered reports of polar bears taking walrus, but these bruins may have been desperately hungry. Whenever the two are together, either they ignore one another or the polar bears give the large tusked bulls a wide berth. A male walrus is nothing to fool with, not even for an adult polar bear.

In Greenland the white bears kill musk-ox and caribou on rare occasions. Russian scientists have seen the bears trying to capture belugas along the edge of the ice of Novaya Zemlya. One bear killed 13 beluga whales that became stranded in a shallow pool created by the ice shifting and breaking up. An 18th-century explorer reported seeing polar bears fishing for salmon in a river of the northern coast of Labrador. But 95 percent or more of the polar bear's diet, year-round, consists of seal meat.

Behavior and intelligence

Naturalists, scientists, and hunters have always tried to determine the intelligence of various wild animals, but that is never easy. Polar bears offer no exception. One measure of animal intelligence may be adaptability to a tough environment, but in polar bears that is either instinctive or learned from the mother. Animal behaviorists believe that intelligence might be measured by the creature's ability to adapt or respond to unusual circumstances. For example, a polar bear that has never seen or smelled a human in its world is suddenly confronted by an Eskimo on a sled drawn by howling dogs. According to Eskimos who have experienced this meeting, most bears quickly turn and run (which seems wisest). An occasional bear will at least make a swift attack on the dogs before running, and a few will stand, perhaps confused, and do nothing at all. The latter invariably are shot.

The coming of researchers

The most radical and abrupt change in the polar bear's world happened in the 1960s and 1970s. All at once, planes and helicopters bearing scientists came roaring out of the skies in search of the animals. But bears seem to have adapted, probably by learning to fear the sound and sight of approaching aircraft.

Sam Miller was among the small corps of biologists who spent many years trying to unlock the mystery of the polar bear's lonely life. According to Miller, a biologist in a helicopter can easily tell if a polar bear has ever been pursued and tranquilized before. If it looks up as it runs away, or stops to look up, it lacks previous experience with wildlife biologists. But if it runs pell-mell and tries to hide, head always down, it has been handled and tagged before. This type will dodge, circle, cut back, and use every conceivable maneuver to stay away from an aircraft. Miller is convinced that some bears become impossible to shoot with a tranquilizing dart because they know when the pilot begins his final swoop for the shot.

Other biologists have seen bears hide under shrubs and tilted ice ridges and they have even seen bears duck into dens or cavities to escape a helicopter. Biologist Charles Jonkel relates seeing one bear dive underwater and stay there to evade capture.

Sam Miller participated in the capture or recapture of about 275 bears during several winters of flying by helicopter and fixed-wing aircraft over Canadian ice pack. The act of searching for the white bears over a white landscape without visible horizon is hazardous enough. But it is impossible to physically handle that many large and powerful animals without experiencing moments of stark terror. Add another ingredient—intense cold—and the job of a polar-bear biologist leaves no room for even small errors. Sam Miller well remembers one nearly fatal mistake.

It was midwinter of 1971. Miller was flying northward along with fellow biologist Ian Stirling and a pilot of the Canadian Wildlife Service. A hundred miles beyond their base at Cape Perry, Northwest Territory, they spotted a female bear with twin cubs. As experience had taught them, they closed in on the fleeing animals and, when near enough, shot a drug-filled dart into the rump of the sow. The bear soon collapsed, and the pilot landed the craft about 200 yards away. Miller cautiously approached the prone sow, with a rifle held ready, until he was convinced that she was completely out. Then he put the .30/06 aside by the helicopter and the team went to work.

First they affixed a numbered metal identification tag in the bruin's ear. Then they tattooed the same number quickly on the bear's lip before its saliva (and the mens' hands) froze. They pulled a premolar tooth to later determine the sow's age. Then they measured and weighed the bear using a cattle girth weight-tape method that is quite accurate. All the while they noticed that one of the cubs kept peeking at them over a nearby ice ridge. They knew that cubs never leave the immediate vicinity of a tranquilized mother. Some remain right at her side even as she is studied and tagged.

When all work had been finished on the female, which required more than an hour, the men turned to catch the curious cub nearby, and walked in that direction. But suddenly the "cub" stood erect and turned out to be a large male they carelessly had not spotted before. It let out a woof and came headlong after them.

Miller drew a handgun he was carrying on his hip and fired over the boar's head. He recalls being startled by the strange muffled sound the pistol made out over the ice pack. The sound made the bear pause for an instant to look behind him, as if he thought the shot had come from that direction. During the ensuing race for the helicopter, the bear actually ran past the men to escape from the danger he thought was behind him.

"The polar acoustics saved our lives," recounted Miller. "After that we never again left a rifle out of reach. And despite the minus 30° F temperature, we were as warm as toast, although weak in the knees, from just a short footrace."

A NOSE FOR TROUBLE

As with other species of bears worldwide, the noses of polar bears too often get them into trouble. They just cannot resist following the scent of food—even the unnatural scent of man's food—to its source. And once at the source, most bears cannot resist trying to obtain it, no matter what the barrier.

In the early days of exploration in the North American Arctic, a simple method was used to attract polar bears into a hunter's point-blank range. A kettle of seal or fish oil was heated over a driftwood fire until it boiled. The oil's scent would waft far out over pack ice or an Arctic island. Soon bears would zero in to that spot, where they would be reduced to pure white bear rugs. From a good location, a hunter might shoot several bears without moving.

Fishing camps, cottages, and garbage dumps in remote Arctic communities are also tempting to the ice bear. From early autumn until freeze-up of Hudson Bay, a good many bears congregate around the village dump outside Churchill, where one can always see them. Dump bears usually become a nuisance, though at Churchill they also provide a benefit. The bears have been extremely easy to capture alive and mark for scientific study without the great expense of chartering aircraft for the purpose. Much about the species has been learned from the Churchill dump bears, but that is an isolated example.

Feeding polar bears, like feeding any of their North American cousins, is asking for serious trouble. Eventually the animals come to expect the handout, and when none is forthcoming they try to take it. One incident aboard a Canadian Coast Guard cutter based in the Arctic provides a good example.

For some time the crew members fed an old male bear by tossing everything from pancakes and peanut butter to meat scraps and molasses bread overboard. The animal grew more and more "tame." Eventually the bear would even stick its head into a porthole begging for more. But one day the cutter was ordered to duty elsewhere and the bruin was left behind with withdrawal problems.

Not much later a second Coast Guard cutter arrived and found a "friendly" polar bear waiting where they anchored. That crew also fed the bear. Still ravenous, the bear climbed aboard via a cargo net and began exploring the ship to find the galley, the source of rich odors. Fire hoses turned on the animal only seemed to amuse it, and the crew eventually had to fire signal-flare rockets to drive it away.

ARE POLAR BEARS DANGEROUS?

During a cruise of remote Arctic outposts in 1976, I talked to a thin, bronzed old man in Pangnirtung, Baffin Island, who showed me frightful scars down his back and buttocks. He had tried to drive away a bear that was killing his sled dogs and it turned on him. A friend who heard the commotion shot the bear when it began to eat his leg. The man seemed to remember it as if it had happened only days ago.

Are polar bears normally dangerous to man? The answer is that they certainly can be. Years ago near Chesterfield Inlet, Northwest Territory, a weathered sign near the Hudson Bay post read, "The only safe polar bear is a distant polar bear." The words "or dead," had been added with a carving knife. Biologist Sam Miller considers polar bears more dangerous than grizzlies. "Many just have no fear of anything," he told me.

Ernest Thompson Seton concluded that polar bears are dangerous because of their unpredictability. John Craighead, a leading grizzly expert with some field observation of polar bears, regards polar bears as less aggressive and less nervous than the grizzlies that he tracked for many years. Ian Stirling believes white bears do not react to humans as quickly as grizzlies. That is also my own opinion. But most agree that three categories of polar bear can be the most lethal: the very hungry bear; the mother bear with cubs; and the suddenly startled bear. Brian Knudsen, a Canadian researcher who studied wildlife on a lonely island in James Bay, northern Ontario, had the bad luck to meet all three of these types of bears.

One evening, a sow with cubs seemed determined to break into Knudsen's shack while he was inside, first by poking her head in the small window, then through a narrow doorway. But unaccountably she turned away and disappeared. Another day while watching a snowy owl, he virtually tripped over a hidden, sleeping bear that backed him, hissing and threatening, all the way to his shack. That bear could easily have killed him, but it also turned away. Still later Knudsen noticed that a lean, arthritic, old female had invaded the island and soon seemed to be stalking him. The bear was not at all afraid of a rifle shot fired close to her. When the tense game went too far, Knudsen shot the bear and found that she was over 30 years old, with only stubs of teeth, and had no chance whatsoever of surviving another winter by catching seals. Her stalking had undoubtedly been motivated by great hunger.

John Hicks, who has been a hunting guide and outfitter, and has live-captured beluga whales in the Churchill River, has had his share of adventures with polar bears. One bruin climbed into a large holding tank and killed a beluga whale that was to be flown to a California marine park. The tank was within the limits of Churchill town. Hicks believes that the barking of dogs can be especially annoying to bears. He reported that a polar bear had killed every dog in a chain of malamutes that belonged to a friend of his at Eskimo Point.

Hicks also told us about the entrepreneur who had started a pig farm on the outskirts of Churchill several years ago. But the man was destined to go out of business quickly—in fact, overnight. One evening, when the white bear migration began from the interior toward the Hudson Bay

coast near Churchill, bears got into the pig pens and carried away every last one of them. Here is an interesting footnote about polar bear behavior: Evidently the animals have a good memory. For years after the pig-pen raid, the bruins returned in search of fresh pork chops. The site of the old pig pen remained a good place to look for a glimpse of the bears for many years.

Speaking of pigs, polar and other bears also may be infected with trichinosis, which is best known as a swine disease. There is even the theory that irritable bears, or bears that attack without provocation, may be suffering the muscular pain of trichinosis. Badly abcessed or decaying teeth might also make a bear very mean.

No year passes without a number of ice-bear attacks reported from the world's polar regions. The animals have attacked men in isolated weather stations, on oil-drilling barges frozen fast in the Beaufort Sea, and at missile tracking facilities. Native people out hunting or trapping may also vanish into the Arctic darkness. But with all of the oil-drilling and other mineral activities now taking place around the North Pole, the number of incidents remains fairly low. The more people come into contact with white bears, however, the more we will read about attacks in the newspapers.

THE ICE BEAR'S GREATEST ENEMY

Except for starvation, which comes with old age, polar bears had no natural enemies and nothing to fear until man invaded their harsh environment. Killer whales may take a swimming bear now and then, but they are not significant predators. Man, then, is the ice bear's greatest enemy.

For a while, it seemed that polar bears might be hunted to extinction as they were pursued everywhere by aircraft and snowmobiles, which gave them no place to run and hide. But although hunting now has virtually stopped, man may be even more threatening.

From 1970 to 1972, Alaskan wildlife researcher Jack Lentfer examined the carcasses of polar bears then taken legally by hunters. He found them to contain low levels of chlorinated hydrocarbons, including dieldrin, endrin, and

In the vicinity of Churchill, Manitoba, some bears have become accustomed to the tracked overland vehicles bearing tourists. Bears, like this one, approach very near, hoping for a food handout.

those of the DDT group. These poisons entered the bears' bodies when the bears ate the seals, which in turn had eaten contaminated aquatic foods carried into polar waters. It is not known if the poison levels have increased in polar bears since 1972, though levels have increased in some Arctic birds. So once again, a species of wildlife is serving as a warning signal to humans that the earth's environment is being damaged.

Even regulated trophy hunting for polar bears will probably never take place again. The population cannot stand the pressure of modern hunting, which frequently involves machines and a whole array of electronic gadgetry. But I have often heard an intriguing proposal from Sam Miller and his fellow biologists who not only know the species best, but have developed a great admiration for the ice bear. "Why not have a year-round open season," one biologist asked, "with-

Some Arctic foxes live parallel lives to polar bears. They may raise young in dens not far from where polar-bear cubs are born. Later some foxes follow bears across the ice and survive all winter long on seal-meat scraps left uneaten by bears.

out any bag limits or having to buy an expensive license, for anyone who wants to go hunting? The only provision would be that the hunter goes out alone, without planes, snowmachines, fire-arms, and walkie-talkies. The man must hunt in the traditional way of Eskimos, with dogs and spears or simple archery equipment. Nothing more."

That kind of hunting would not make even a small dent in the world's polar bear population, although it probably would put a small dent in the hunter population.

Except for man, the orca, or killer whale, is the polar bear's only potential natural enemy. The great white bruins are vulnerable to orca attack when they swim the sometimes long distance between Arctic ice floes.

CHAPTER 5
OTHER WILDLIFE

Grizzlies of the northern Rocky Mountains may at times be seen digging for Uinta ground squirrels, locally called chiselers. This squirrel is giving the frantic alarm call it might give when a bruin comes into view.

I f you have ever seen a black bear suddenly stop grazing or traveling across country and vigorously scratch itself, the bear may be bothered by one of countless other creatures that share the bruin's world. These creatures range in size from nearly invisible chiggers to killer whales weighing more than a ton. They include birds, reptiles, and fish, as well as insects and mammals. In this case, the bear was probably scratching chiggers. And the chances are good that you would be scratching too if you were in the same area.

Chiggers are among the strangest, most bothersome insects a bruin might ever encounter. They are really mites, and are related to ticks. Perhaps because they have no love life, chiggers of North America are downright mean. The male crawls about in grass and bush, very often in berry patches that bears frequent, leaving small packets of sperm in its wake. The female also wanders about and engulfs the first packet she finds. She then attaches herself to the first living thing to come along, which might be the foot of a bear, or a bear photographer.

When a chigger female finds a good tasty spot on the body, usually in an embarrassing location, the chigger sinks a pair of piercing jaws, called *chelicerae*, into the skin. Contrary to popular belief, the chiggers do not suck blood; instead they eat skin, secreting saliva with a potent enzyme that breaks down skin cells. Chiggers feast, sometimes for days, until

If you hike through a western forest and suddenly flush several Steller's jays all at once, you just may be approaching a bear's food cache—usually an animal carcass. The jays are a warning to proceed carefully or, better still, to back off.

they are full. The result is a terrible itching, which any afflicted bear must stop and vigorously scratch. A lot of chigger "bites" might even make the bear irritable.

When working in bear country, I have had my share of chigger bites, which can be prevented by spraying outer garments with insect repellent, and later by washing with strong soap. But black flies and mosquitos have been an even greater torment. In fact, I fear hordes of both hummers far more than I do any bears I've ever met. More than once when filming bears during spring in northern Michigan and Minnesota, the combination of black flies and mosquitos constantly buzzing about my face and bare hands almost drove me from the field. Only modern chemical repellents keep the devils away.

Black flies seem to torment black bears most during the early summer, which is the peak of the bug's abundance. I have seen bears repeatedly brush them away from the face and eyes, eventually running away from the area of concentration. Later, when I projected my slides of those same black bears onto a screen, I could clearly see the swarm of hovering black flies.

Mosquitos are tiny, delicate, nectar-sipping insects that would be almost innocuous, except for the fact that females must also sip blood protein to reproduce. Not many living things escape the preying females, which go after bruins and man alike. Male mosquitos are harmless. In Alaska, where the stupefying cold and snow of winter suddenly change to summer warmth and green mountainsides, I have seen mosquitos appear in clouds all at once. This may actually have some great effect on bear behavior—or on where they wander—but I've never found any scientific evidence to prove it. Still, this overwhelming sub-Arctic hummer is an important factor in any bear's world.

THE RODENTS

Many creatures that share the bear's world are extremely important to bears as prey, while others compete with bears for food. Some creatures have played a major role in changing the bear's habitat. Others, such as the handsome Steller's jay, the chipmunk, and the hyperactive red squirrel, or

This least chipmunk is eating the seeds of mountain ash, a plant which brightens the northern and mountain landscapes in October. Chipmunks are a part of bear habitat almost everywhere.

Beavers have always altered bear habitat in America with their dams, temporarily for the worse, in time for the better. Rarely, a wandering bear might catch a beaver cutting wood too far from the safety of water.

Because the grizzly bear's world has diminished to a few mountain strongholds, prairie dogs are no longer a part of it. But there are many old reports of bruins digging in prairie-dog towns when the big animals still roamed freely over the Great Plains.

chickaree, are simply part of the scenery.

Beavers have altered and shaped the North American environment perhaps more than any other mammal except man. They gnaw down softwood thickets and even small forests to dam up waterways and create ponds. In the center of the pond the rodents usually build a safe and dry lodge that can be entered only through an underwater entrance. Beaver dams can be quite impressive in all dimensions. I have seen dams as long as a football field, and strong enough to support a man on horseback crossing from one end to the other. Almost any beaver dam is a marvel of natural engineering and diligence.

The ponds created by beaver dams have been beneficial to some animals, such as moose, which graze on aquatic vegetation; but the flooding may also have caused a temporary loss of bear habitat. Later, as the ponds fill with silt, meadows are created and bears can find edible plants here once again.

Both black and grizzly bears may prey on beavers when they find the animals cutting wood far

from the safety of water. Young beavers, driven from home to find their own territories, may fall victim to a bear if the two paths happen to cross. I have also read reports of both grizzlies and blacks climbing onto beaver houses and trying to dig out the occupants. Although the bears are sometimes successful, these attempts do not happen frequently. But if a bear ever does manage to trap an adult beaver in its home, it will have a substantial meal. Depending on age and location, beavers weigh from 30 to 80 pounds or more.

Other rodents are far more important than beavers to the day-to-day lives of many bears. The several species of ground squirrels are among the most appealing creatures anyone passing through grizzly-bear country is likely to meet. They are numerous, busy, and uninhibited, and are fascinating to watch. In my backyard is a colony of the same Uinta ground squirrels, locally called chiselers, that the black bears of Grand Teton and the grizzlies of Yellowstone dig up at every opportunity. One of the best indications that bears have visited a vicinity is the bare earth freshly excavated around ground-squirrel colonies. I have no idea exactly how fruitful the digging is, but it must produce a worthwhile tidbit now and then. Late in summer—when the squirrel population is highest, and when young-of-the-year squirrels are establishing their own satellite underground colonies—seems to be when Rocky Mountain grizzlies do the most searching and digging.

At the beginning of the 19th century, when grizzlies still roamed the American Great Plains, the bears often frequented prairie-dog towns. They might still do so today, except that there are no longer any places where grizzlies and prairie dogs still coexist.

One autumn, I watched two different grizzlies of Denali National Park hunt for Arctic ground squirrels, or siksiks. At the northern latitudes beyond the timberline, where they live, siksiks have only a very brief summer in which to eat, raise a family, and accumulate enough body fat to survive the long Alaskan winter in hibernation. Thus by late summer, most Arctic ground-squirrels become roly-poly and slow afoot. If an agile grizzly finds a siksik gorging on Arctic "hay" at this time of year, the bear can often catch it. If anyone ever doubts the speed and sudden acceleration of grizzlies, he should watch them pursue siksiks at Sable Pass on an autumn afternoon.

Marmots, which are larger rodents than ground squirrels, also are taken by bears. In fact some digging on mountainsides may be for marmots, close cousins to the eastern groundhog, rather than for ground squirrels. Both the yellow-bellied marmots of the northern Rocky Mountains and the hoary marmots of British Columbia and Alaska are extremely alert creatures. When they're not safely underground—often beneath rock slides where digging out would be difficult—they sit on rocky points that offer a view all around. When trouble approaches in the form of a bear or a circling golden eagle, the marmot emits a shrill whistle as it scrambles for cover. The whistle warns all other marmots within hearing.

On one memorable sunny morning, Peggy and I sat in the center of a cluster of marmot holes on Hurricane Ridge, high in Olympic National Park. Several of the marmots were in sight watching us as we focused telephoto lenses on them from close range. These particular marmots had become accustomed to hikers passing on nearby trails, and were not uneasy about our presence. One seemed very curious. But without warning, an alert marmot whistled and all vanished in the next second. At first we couldn't understand the abrupt alarm, but as we stood up to stretch we spotted the young black bear that was working its way closer around the ridge. The marmots did not re-emerge until the bruin was almost out of sight.

Years ago some dedicated scientist counted the number of quills on a porcupine and came up with an estimated total of 26,000. Wildlife rangers in British Columbia recently live-trapped a troublesome female black bear and found her to have about 24 quills embedded in her muzzle. That was puzzling, because most bears are smart enough never to molest porcupines, which they might meet quite often. After the men had tranquilized the sow and removed the quills, they may have solved the mystery.

Nearby was a small cub that was thin and whimpering, seemingly in pain because it resembled a small black pincushion. The rangers believe that the cub had somehow run afoul of a porcupine and may even have tried to play with it. The mother bear probably rushed to the cub's aid and was also quilled. Normally bears and porcupines live segregated lives by mutual agreement; but porcupines may change bear habitat by girdling the trunks of some trees in a forest and thereby killing them.

THE DEER FAMILY

It is difficult to think of bears and not also consider all the members of the North American deer family. I always visualize whitetail deer in black-bear country, and vice versa, although the range of the black bear today does not match the great range of the eastern whitetail. For many years, the only black bears I ever saw were those observed from a deer stand or those driven past my stand during an early season whitetail hunt. It always seemed to me that black bears were a lot more wary and owned keener senses than the whitetails they lived with, which is saying quite a lot for a bear's senses.

Black bears wandering in springtime will inevitably come upon whitetail fawns that have been left alone while the mothers feed; these fawns will quickly be killed and eaten at this time of year when animal protein is scarce. Some older bears may hunt specifically for whitetail fawns during that period when the fawns are not yet following the mother. A Michigan pulpwood logger told me that he once watched a medium-size black bear trying to catch a fawn, which could run on wobbly legs, but was having a hard time keeping away from the bear. He did not know how the chase ended.

Both grizzlies and western black bears occupy typical range of the mule deer, elk, and Shiras (Wyoming) moose. Both bears will also capture fawns and calves of these species if they have the opportunity, and both will suffer if the range is ever overgrazed by too many deer or domestic livestock. Good mule deer country and good elk country also tends to be good bear country.

When they emerge from hibernation, in some areas, especially where elk are concentrated in winter yards or on "feed grounds," bears may depend on these winter-weakened animals as a source of food. The same is true in southeastern Alaska, where brown bears may kill a good many blacktail deer, left in poor condition by the typically cold, damp winter and an undersupply of nutritious natural forage. But as powerful and quick as bears are, they are not normally able to catch elk, deer, or moose in prime condition.

In Alaska, the Yukon, and the Northwest Territory, grizzlies share the vast wilderness with barren-ground caribou. In Alaska's Denali National Park, I have often seen the two in the same area, apparently ignoring one another. But I am certain that if a caribou revealed any sign that it was very sick or injured, and lagging behind the herd, most bears would surely take notice. Grizzlies have been seen killing huge caribou bulls, but these might have been males already injured in rutting combat. More often than not, a grizzly will drive wolves away from their caribou kill rather than make the kill on its own. The same is true of kills of Dall, Stone, and bighorn sheep. Grizzlies do roam widely and freely in wild sheep range, but capturing a healthy ram or ewe would seem out of the question. Although I have also seen grizzlies and mountain goats not far apart,

Whitetail-deer country and black-bear country are virtually the same over much of America. In fact, a very quiet deer-stalker is the person most likely to see a black bear.

it is even more unlikely that a bear could ever catch a healthy goat (even a kid), which is the most surefooted of North American big-game species.

Early one summer morning in northwestern Wyoming, I sat on a gravel bank overlooking a beaver pond, waiting for a cow moose and calf to emerge from shadows into the golden sunlight. Eventually they appeared. Both waded out into the center of the impoundment, where the cow began dipping her homely muzzle into the water to nibble on fresh green shoots. The small calf stood right next to its mother. As I aimed a camera at the pair, I saw the female raise her head suddenly as if in alarm. Then she stood sniffing in the opposite direction, as if uncertain whether to leave the pond or stay. A few minutes later I spotted the reason for the concern; a black bear with a cub was walking along a brushy game trail that led toward the beaver pond.

I checked all the camera exposure settings with nervous hands, especially when the bear stopped in her tracks and half-stood up on hind legs for a better look ahead. I was ready to focus on any dramatic encounter that might take place. But in the next instant the two bears turned and disappeared in another direction, while the moose and calf also waded out of the water and away. It was a fine example of mutual avoidance.

An adult moose is formidable prey, even under the most favorable circumstances. The largest members of the world's deer family, bull moose can easily weigh 1,200 pounds. When compared to elk and deer, a moose may appear ungainly and ponderous. Its deep and heavy body is mounted on stiltlike legs. The long face features a drooping muzzle that only a mother moose could love. But the moose is a strong evolutionary jewel perfectly suited to survive wherever it lives. Only a very desperate bear would be foolish enough to tackle a cow moose with a young calf. For the most part, bears and moose get along well together; and he who sees both species at once is lucky indeed.

BISON

Bruins that long ago excavated in prairie-dog towns depended far more on very old and very

In some regions, grizzly bears have been blamed for high mortality among moose calves. But a bruin would wisely detour around a giant Alaskan bull such as this one coming into the rutting season.

A Dall ram dozes in warm August sunshine on a rocky bed high in the Alaska Range. From its lofty vantage-point, it should be able to see at least one grizzly bear on the landscape below.

Next pages: A wet spring snow is falling on this Shiras moose bull in northwestern Wyoming. Soon all the bears in the area will be emerging from winter sleeping quarters.

Weasels are fairly common creatures that we do not see too often. I filmed this short-tailed weasel in an area of Glacier National Park much favored by grizzly bears.

Raccoons are abundant in the world of the black bear, especially in the Southeast. Although the two eat many of the same foods, there is no significant competition between them.

This river otter has just captured a brook trout from beneath a partially frozen beaver pond in Wyoming. Peggy and I watched a party of three otters catch eight trout in this spot on a bright November morning.

young stragglers from the great bison herds that ranged from Texas northward into Canada. Old accounts describe how a bear might run down a bison that was not quite able to keep up with its companions. Just as often a bear might drive prairie wolves away from their kill. Wherever bears and wolves exist together, they are in competition for the same prey.

Nowadays in Yellowstone Park, grizzlies are again feeding on the rapidly expanding buffalo herd. The dead are mostly animals weakened by age or the bitter winter, or struck by cars on the park highway. Find a bison carcass anywhere, and a bear is almost certain to be nearby. At least two of the bear-man encounters in Yellowstone one recent year occurred when hikers (in one instance a park naturalist and his wife) came suddenly upon a bison carcass being guarded by a bear. The bear attacked and injured the couple in defense of the carcass.

PHOTOGRAPHER'S BONUSES

Peggy and I have met many residents of the bear's world while photographing or watching bears. Once a short-tailed weasel appeared practically at the base of my tripod as I concentrated on the much larger animal far away. We have found river otters catching brook trout at the beaver pond where we were examining the fresh tracks of a black bear. Tiny rabbitlike pikas harvested hay on the edge of a rock avalanche area where we watched a black bear wolfing down huckleberries, branches and all. Ravens have called our attention to bears we might never have seen. Chickadees are common birds of bear habitat, and so are all of the forest species of grouse: ruffed, blue, and spruce. The latter are often so tame when encountered by a photographer that it seems a quick bruin would be able to catch one on the ground. The sleek, seldom-seen pine marten is another bonus species we have encountered more than once while out searching for bears.

OTHER PREDATORS

All bears, even the great white bruins of the Arctic, share their habitat with other predators— some on an intimate, almost symbiotic basis, oth-

ers only distantly. Cougars or mountain lions are in the latter category. Especially in the American Southwest, a hunter following a pack of hound dogs is just as likely to strike a black bear as a cougar track. Many years ago, while pursuing the trail of a large, sheep-eating black bear in Utah, the hounds I was following were diverted by a fresh spoor that crossed the bear track. Some of the younger dogs turned and followed it.

After an hour of tough and sweaty climbing, in a canyon cul-de-sac, we reached the place where the hounds had treed a female cougar with a half-grown cougar cub. These were the first of only five cougars I have ever seen in a lifetime spent in the wild, much of it in cougar country. We collected the dogs, left the two cats unharmed in the tree, and went back to the original bear trail.

But too much time was lost, and we never caught up to that particular elusive bruin that seemed to vanish in another box canyon. Black bears have a way of doing that. According to Willis Buttolph, an old-time professional lion and bear hunter in central Utah's Green River country, black bears of the canyonlands are a lot tougher to track and bring to bay than the cougars that also live in that region.

Gray wolves also live with bears over vast areas of northern North American wilderness. Wolves are predators that hunt in packs, but I have found numerous accounts of grizzly bears driving a whole pack away from their kills. There have also been reports of wolves successfully defending carcasses from bears. The disputes, however, almost always end without serious injury to either. Final possession is settled by obvious superiority, by overwhelming numbers, or by bluffing.

During spring in Yellowstone Park, coyotes often find the carcasses of winter-killed elk and bison before bears do. In fact coyotes may succeed in eating much of an animal before a bear ever arrives. But once a bear reaches the scene, there is no question about possession. Perhaps

Next pages: Grizzlies of the Great Plains killed and ate bison, which existed in astronomical numbers. Today grizzlies are again feeding on the proliferating buffaloes of Yellowstone National Park.

It is midwinter and bears are sleeping in underground beds. But this one common native of bear country—the coyote—continues to hunt over the deep snow.

The paths of bears and gray wolves are bound to cross wherever the animals exist together. I have seen both at the same time in Denali National Park. But neither animal seeks the other's company.

no sound better symbolizes bear country and the whole American wilderness than a symphony of coyotes howling on a clear, cold night.

In my own experience, foxes more than any other mammal have seemed to be closely associated with bears. In Denali National Park, you are likely to see red foxes in those same areas where you are most likely to encounter grizzlies. Year after year, red foxes dig dens and raise kits at Sable Pass, which is one area of greatest grizzly density. The main reason for the presence of both is the dependable annual crop of berries and ground squirrels that both foxes and bears relish.

Quite often we have found foxes living along the major Alaskan salmon streams where brown bears gather every summer. The foxes feed on fish scraps and salmon eggs scattered by the bruins. I have also seen red-fox parents dragging whole salmon to feed kits at their den near Chenik Creek. But I do not know if the fox actually caught the salmon or if the fish was discarded

by a bear (which is more likely). One time I watched a wolf trying to catch spawning fish in the American River just outside Katmai National Park. A group of seven wolves then frequented the area where brown bears did most of their fishing at night. On several early mornings I watched wolves in the same shallow spot gleaning the scraps.

Of all foxes, none live in a harsher environment than Arctic foxes of the far North, which wear a pure white pelage during the winter. Some Arctic foxes manage to survive the long, dark, intensely cold season simply by following polar bears as they wander, hunting, across the ice pack. For several months, these foxes must travel over unfamiliar territory where temperatures fall far below zero, eating only the leftovers of seals not entirely consumed by polar bears. That means the pickings are usually slim. During the summer, Arctic fox kits might be eaten by bears that come across their dens, which are dug between the

Cougars, or mountain lions, share black-bear range in many wilderness areas of the West and Southwest. Both can be troublesome to livestock owners. No more beautiful symbol of the western canyon-country exists than this sleek and tawny cat.

permafrost and the tundra surface.

BOBCATS

I have also associated bobcats with black bear country (and lynx with grizzly country) ever since the time I saw both during the same trip to the Okefenokee Swamp in 1954. One morning a bruin swam across a narrow alligator run directly in the path of our canoe. Several nights later a bobcat ran across a forest trail, illuminated by the headlights of our car. But that was not just happenstance. The range of the black bear and the natural range of the bobcat nearly coincide.

If any common mammal is more shy or more reclusive than the black bear, it is the eastern bobcat. Except when trapped or treed by hounds, bobcats simply are not seen. I have never seen one east of the Mississippi River in broad daylight. Furthermore, the species does not have that

The bobcat, like the whitetail deer, has a natural range that almost matches that of the black bear.

We have often found red foxes sharing the same areas with brown and grizzly bears, especially in Alaska. Often the foxes are scavengers of bear food sources, namely salmon and animal carcasses.

In winter, adult Arctic foxes follow polar bears across Arctic ice to survive on seal scraps left by the bears. But if a bear found these kits in their den, it would eat them, too.

major weakness common to most bears—an attraction to human or unnatural food sources. The bobcat just may be the wariest dweller of the black bear's world.

Opossums

Broadly speaking, virtually all common species of bird or mammal sometime and somewhere shares the world of the bear. In the southeastern United States, a family of raccoons or opossums may live in a tree den in the same forest, or possibly in the same old hollow hickory tree, in which a black bear discovers a wild beehive. Opossums are notorious carrion eaters, a trait they share with black bears. A night-wandering bruin might also obtain an unexpected warm meal if it happens to intercept a family of opossums out foraging on the ground. One likely place for the two species to meet might be in a woodland where persimmon and pawpaw fruits are ripe and fragrant in late fall.

The opossum is another of those creatures native to the black bear's domain. Because it is nocturnal, the opossum is not often seen. This one was filmed in a flowering redbud tree.

BIRDS

Many different birds, some common and some rare, some plain and some very colorful, have always made wandering through the bear's world even more interesting. For one thing, Peggy and I are serious birdwatchers, a full-time hobby that has trained us to be much better wildlife finders and observers overall. We have been able to spot bears on distant mountainsides, probably because our eyes have become accustomed to spotting small details such as the field marks on wood warblers and flycatchers.

Some of the most obvious bear-country birds are the gulls and jays and bald eagles that gather wherever bruins feed on spawning fish. We also associate other birds and bird activities with certain bear seasons. For example, when rose-breasted grosbeaks (and any number of other songbirds) are singing their springtime courtship songs in woodlands of the northern Midwest, look for black bears to begin shedding last year's

We have often met pine martens, although nowhere really abundant, in areas of the northern Rockies where both black bears and grizzlies exist.

Wild turkeys—like whitetails, squirrels, and ruffed grouse—are familiar in the eastern black bear's territory. Turkeys also subsist on some of the same foods that bears eat: acorns, seeds, fruits, and berries.

In the bleak, remote nesting areas of emperor geese in western Alaska, brown bears have been observed eating the goslings, as well as the young of other nesting waterfowl and shorebirds.

long fur coat. Willow ptarmigan start to slowly exchange their white winter plumage for red-brown summer feathers at about the same time grizzly bears emerge from hibernation. One of the best times to spot an itinerant black bear in the Southeast is when tom turkeys begin strutting and gobbling in hardwood openings. Sit quietly and motionless near the male turkeys, and the next black shadow you see, if you're below the Mason-Dixon Line, might be that of a black bear.

One of the great wildlife migrations on earth is the mass flight of waterfowl and shorebirds back from wintering in the southern United States (and from as far away as southern South America) to nest in the Arctic. It is hard to comprehend, without actually seeing it, how many birds are suddenly concentrated on previously barren landscapes of Alaska and Canada. Both polar bears and barren-ground grizzlies dine extensively on fowl protein during this short, fast nesting period, when eggs may be exposed and some young birds are unable to escape. One day on a remote Arctic island, Canadian biologist Sten Hansen watched a polar bear eat the goslings in three nests, a brood of snowy owls, and the eggs or chicks in three unidentified shorebird nests, in rapid succession. Alaskan brown bears have been observed lumbering about in an Arctic tern colony, wolfing down as many eggs or downy chicks as they could find.

For several years, Alaskan wildlife biologist Ed Bailey and his associate Nina Faust have made a survey-census of nesting seabirds on each of the hundreds of offshore islands of the Alaska Peninsula and the Aleutian Islands. It is a massive and often a hazardous undertaking. The exploration is possible only in an outboard-powered inflatable raft (which can be landed on small rock piles), and it must often be done in the foulest weather and through turbulent passages to make the lonely beachheads. This work has been absolutely the highest kind of outdoor adventure.

Bailey and Faust have also had some thrills they didn't anticipate. More than once on remote islands far from the Alaskan mainland, they have been surprised to find brown bears, some of them unfriendly. And, more than once, the pair have had to make a hasty retreat into an angry sea. The biologists concluded that there was only one possible explanation for finding the bears so far from their normal haunts: The bruins were living on the young birds and eggs of the rookeries of puffins, kittiwakes, murres, guillemots, shearwaters, and petrels.

MARINE MAMMALS

The edge of the sea environment also brings brown bears and ice bears into close contact with many of the marine mammals. Once along the cold shore of Afognak Island, Roy Randall, Peggy, and I watched a brown bear feeding on the carcass of a Steller's sea lion. We do not know if the sea lion simply washed ashore already dead of other causes or if the bear was able to stalk and kill the animal when it hauled out on the rocky banks.

Harbor seals, which are fairly common along inlets and on countless islands along the Alaskan coast, might also become brown-bear prey. Farther north, especially after Arctic seas have partially frozen, polar bears may be able to stalk walruses as well as the seals that are their normal fare. I mention this because of a photograph we took of one bull walrus on Akpatok Island, north of Hudson Bay. The walrus has a deep gash across the top of its head, and claw marks on its flanks, which might only have been incurred in an encounter with a polar bear. Besides that, polar bears are known to frequent Akpatok Island.

BEAR LONGEVITY

Once they become adults, the bears of North America have no real natural enemies except for parasites, tapeworms, and other internal creatures that sap a bruin's strength. If they are not shot or otherwise eliminated by people, bears eventually perish from old age and/or starvation. Teeth are worn down beyond their ability to chew enough nutritious food. A kind of bear arthritis sets in, and strength vanishes from the great bodies. Some biologists believe that very old bears just never emerge from their winter dens.

KILLER WHALES

Some polar bears, however, may have to fear one predator that is even larger and more potentially dangerous: the killer whale.

I have read old translated accounts by Scandinavian whaling captains that describe killer whales attacking polar bears as they swam from ice floe to ice floe. Of course that is a real possibility, and the accounts may well be true. But there is reason to doubt other stories of killer whales stalking polar bears walking along a frozen shoreline or an iceberg. One Norwegian observer claimed that he saw a killer whale raise its head out of the water to accurately locate a white bear on an ice floe. The whale then tipped the floe upside down, throwing the bear into the water where it was torn to bloody bits by a whole pod of whales.

Whether that story is true or not, the killer whale is the only animal sharing the bear's world that might also prey on bears with any regularity. No such creature exists on land. If our native bears are to survive in their world, it is in our human hands.

Polar bears may at times be able to prey on walruses when the walruses have hauled out onto shore or onto ice floes. I once saw a walrus with a deep head wound that may have escaped from either a polar bear or a killer whale. I saw it on Akpatok Island in the Canadian Arctic, which is frequented throughout summer by the white bears.

CHAPTER 6

BEARS AND PEOPLE

Bear-human confrontations are bound to occur when people invade the wilderness in large numbers. Many bears eventually learn that backpackers carry easily available food. This grizzly is pawing through a pack discarded by a frightened trail hiker.

The Great Ontario Bear Hunt of 1960 stimulated a lot of bitter controversy and protest, but it proceeded as planned. The forces of reason and conversation do not win often enough in Canada or the United States.

It all started when the tall furred hats—worn by the guards at London's Buckingham Palace—were beginning to look ragged, moth-eaten, and not at all imperial. Leo Del Villano, mayor of Timmins, northern Ontario, offered to supply as many bearskins as necessary to rehat the royal guards. About 300 would be enough. The hunt began on May 16 when the surrounding forests became clear of snow and the bruins emerged from hibernation. The pelts would be at their finest and glossiest then. Teams of hunters combed the woods in search of black bears, large and small. As might be expected, hunters as well as nonhunters reacted angrily at a bear slaughter for such an idiotic purpose. After all, imitation bear fur could have been used to restore the shakos. But the Ontario government meekly elected not to interfere.

No matter from which side it is viewed, the hunt was not a success. Only 62 bears were killed, which was an embarrassment for Mayor Del Villano. Yet this small number was enough to seriously deplete the bear population in the Timmins region for years thereafter. One officer of Ontario's Lands and Forests Department later admitted that during the hunt many more bears were only wounded by inexperienced gunners, and

Street signs such as this one in Churchill, Manitoba, have helped to reduce the number of bear-people incidents that once threatened to eliminate the bears.

selling not only ungdam, but claws, paws, hides, and cuts of meat to the burgeoning Asian community around Los Angeles. One guide was caught in a sting operation when he sold 187 claws and gall bladders to an undercover agent. The guide could earn more money poaching than he could taking out a sportsman client.

The legal harvest of black bears in California was 766 in 1981, but authorities believe that the illegal kill for sale of bear parts at least equaled that figure.

Consider a few revealing details of the California investigation. One Korean buyer ordered 300 bear paws, 14 gall bladders, plus cougar galls from each of five different professional guides. The paws were supplied to Chinese restaurants where they sold for $30 each and were considered epicurean fare. Lately the supply network for black-bear parts has extended as far north as British Columbia and as far east as Wisconsin, and includes all of the West. Traveling toward the Northwest from Los Angeles on a major buying trip, one dealer had spent all his money for ungdam and other bear parts by the time he reached Sacramento.

The illegal poaching of black bears is doubly sad because of the earlier loss of the California grizzly. Although the state flag still depicts the once-numerous grizzly, death came to the last one in California at the hands of Jess B. Agnew at Horse Corral Meadow, Fresno County, in August 1922.

California scientists are not yet concerned that someone will someday shoot the last black bear. But they are gravely concerned about a decline in breeding that could result in an eventual collapse of the population. Black bears mature sexually at four and one half years. The average age of bears taken legally in the state is also four and one half years, which is similar to Idaho and other western areas where the animals are heavily pursued as game. But the growing demand for ungdam and bear parts results in more and more black bears being shot before they have a chance to breed. Many are poached in spring when the gall bladders are the largest. In 1984, poachers were found using a small explosive device packed with sodium cyanide to kill bears for gall bladders. The same devices could also kill people who stumble upon them.

Fortunately when writing about men and bears, there is some good news to be woven into the bad. Let's go back briefly to 1982.

POLAR-BEAR WATCHERS AND BEAR JAILS

It is a late October evening in Churchill, Manitoba, when a group of parka-clad tourists gathers in the lounge of the Arctic Inn to watch a National Geographic Society film about polar bears photographed in this very place. Jim Macleod, genial proprietor of the lodging, is busy focusing the projector when his wife, Rita, sweeps in.

"There's a bear," she says, "just beyond our lobby."

Everyone rushes to the door to have a look. Outside, dry snow is falling on the dark and deserted street. Down the middle of the street walks a large white bruin, eerily illuminated by greenish lights coming from the Hudson Bay store just across the street. The travelers have just arrived by jet plane from Winnipeg, 700 miles south, and this is the first polar bear any of them have seen except in confinement. They watch it in disbelief until a Royal Canadian Mounted Police pickup truck, blue and red lights flashing, appears out of the night. The troopers use firecrackers to drive the bear out of town toward the rocky headland of Cape Merry.

That is only the beginning. Before the week-long trip ends, everyone will have watched or aimed their cameras at as many as 50 or more bears, often at very close range. During the past decade or two, adventuresome tourists have discovered a number of great wildlife spectacles around the world from the Serengeti Plain in Tanzania to Yellowstone and the Galapagos. All are popular today, but few can match the strange bear "show" that takes place where the Churchill River empties into Hudson Bay in extreme northeastern Manitoba, when the days become short.

Every fall, after a summer of fasting and indolence on the vast and desolate tundra south of Churchill, the bears are drawn toward the coastline to await the annual freeze-up of the bay, which we have described earlier. The bruins are hungry for the seals that they will soon be able to stalk out on the ice pack. It is during these two to five weeks the bears spend waiting in the Churchill region that scientists can best study, mark, and evaluate the species. The Churchill region is also virtually the only place on earth where ordinary people can easily see one of the most magnificent of large creatures living in the wild.

The annual gathering of bears has been a mixed blessing to the 700 permanent residents of Churchill because the animals once were a dreaded problem. In the past they have broken into homes, camps, and food caches. In 1968 a young boy was mauled and killed. A number of others have been injured. Nuisance bears have been trapped in backyards, playgrounds, and on the parking lot of the Catholic Eskimo museum. Everyone in town has at least one humorous or hair-raising bear story to tell.

Typical is the incident of the local drunk who staggers out of a bar on a bitter November night and suddenly comes face to face with a bear out in the street. According to a friend: "He set a new Canadian speed record for sobering up, as well as for running, and has been sober ever since."

Churchill is no doubt the only community on earth where parents and armed motor patrols accompany children trick-or-treating on Halloween night. It may also have the only large airport where landing aircraft must watch out for the white bears on the tarmac, and where one animal broke into a hangar and ate an entire cargo of doughnuts just shipped in from Winnipeg. But despite the potential danger, the so-called polar bear problem is mostly under control today. In 1970, 20 bears were destroyed in the interest of public safety. Now, because of a cooperative public alert and alarm system, plus a good dose of education, a whole year may pass without a single bear being killed in self defense.

Most Churchill townspeople are at least philosophical about their predicament. Some are now proud of the bears, and many residents are prospering from what has evolved into a bonanza. They sell bumper stickers and T-shirts that brag about the "polar bear capitol of the world," and proclaim, "our only house pests are polar bears." Now the daily train and at least three weekly flights from Winnipeg bring thousands of tourists every autumn to see the bear show.

Although Peggy and I have photographed polar bears elsewhere in the Arctic, we returned to Churchill for the third time because there simply is no better opportunity anywhere for snapping the white bears. Among other photographer-scientists on hand were the New York Zoological Society's Dr. George Schaller with his wife, back from studying pandas in China; Dr. Ian Stirling, chief researcher of the Canadian Wildlife Service; and Dr. Dan Guravich, leading one of several groups of touring naturalists.

Transportation across the frozen landscape, over which very few roads have been built, is by bus, by tracked all-terrain snow coach, or by tundra wagon. The last is a huge, double-decker bus-size vehicle with balloon tires, which can easily carry up to 30 people to wherever the bruins are most concentrated at any given time. Peggy and I opted to have our own four-wheel-drive pickup transported to Churchill by train, just for the extra convenience.

Photographers can easily find subjects simply by driving eastward out of town and parallel to the shore of Hudson Bay. The first groups of bears were usually found digging into garbage around the town dump, sometimes right next to piles of burning trash. But many of these animals had large numbers painted on their sides for identification by scientists, and we had no interest in them.

A few miles farther, the surf had piled slush and seaweed high on the beach, and we usually found bears loitering here. Often they would swim out in the freezing water as if in training for the seal-hunting season ahead. It was a great place to set up and shoot because of the high angle from roadside directly down onto the subject. Another advantage of the elevation was the safety, because it is foolish to approach very near on foot. We spent many fascinating hours there watching the antics of cubs through a viewfinder and long telephoto lens. One sow we discovered along the beach with three cubs, each nearly as large as herself, was an old friend. We had photographed that same female a year before when the cubs were much smaller and less menacing. One cub kept stalking me mischievously wherever I set up a tripod.

Perhaps more than some other large mammals, all white bears did not react the same way to motor vehicles and photographers. Some would let us approach very closely (or approach *us* very closely), while others would vanish at first encounter, or at least keep a distance too far for even a long telephoto lens to be used.

Our favorite subjects were three medium-size male bears we usually found together somewhere around a chain of frozen, freshwater ponds. Some days we discovered them sleeping on the open ice, but more often they were standing erect, play-fighting, and swinging with both forelegs. Any wildlife photographer relishes that kind of live, lasting action. It is amazing how the bears can sustain such vigorous exercise for days on end while eating next to nothing.

The three bears were still sparring playfully when Hudson Bay finally froze solid in mid-November. The very next morning, there was not a single polar bear left on land near Churchill, Manitoba. The photographers and tourists headed southward, and innkeeper Jim Macleod pondered expanding his Arctic Inn to better handle a new wave of bear watchers expected the next fall.

During fall 1983, the truce between Churchill people and polar bears was somewhat strained. Late one bitter night, a local restaurant caught fire and burned. Inside the structure was a large freezer full of fresh meat. After the fire had burned out, a local Cree Indian man poked through the ruins, found the thawed, half-cooked meat in the freezer, and stuffed the pockets of his parka with it. Walking toward home on the edge of town, he was attacked and killed by a bear, which almost certainly had been attracted to the smell of the meat. The bear was then shot.

At almost the same time, Dan Guravich was in a balloon-tired tundra buggy with a party of photographers across the tundra southeast of Churchill. From the start of the trip, the party had been seeing plenty of bears, many of which came very close to the huge vehicle, even walking underneath and around it. At night, a young bruin rocked awake the campers inside by bumping the wheel mounts. During several earlier trips, the animals had learned that there would be scraps of food wherever the buggy traveled. In fact, bears were baited to come nearer, so the occupants might photograph better. Such familiarity breeds contempt. But the people inside the buggy had no reason whatever to feel insecure, protected by their metal capsule.

On Thanksgiving day a blizzard raged outside the buggy, with Arctic winds gusting to 65 mph. At 10:30 A.M. somebody spotted an ivory gull, extremely rare in that area. All took positions at open windows with their cameras to film the bird. One of the men, Fred Treul of Milwaukee, extended his left arm out a window to steady his camera as he concentrated on the gull through a telephoto lens. The next sound he heard above the wind was the crunch of his elbow bones in the jaws of a polar bear.

The bear, a large aggressive male previously seen around the vehicle, hung on grimly for several seconds until beaten in the face by the others aboard. Because of the savage blizzard, it was impossible to send a helicopter from Churchill to pick up Treul. One rescue vehicle broke down en route overland, but another somehow drove through the storm. After a terribly rough ride and much floundering in snowdrifts, Treul reached a hospital in shock, but eventually recovered. He

Tracked all-terrain vehicles carry tourists to see polar bears on the tundra surrounding Churchill, Manitoba.

holds no grudge against the bear, which permanently damaged his arm, or against bears in general. He cites his own carelessness and concedes that the bruin was blameless.

The blizzard ended soon after the mauling incident of Thanksgiving Day. Next night, as the northern lights bathed Churchill in an eerie glow, a female bear with twin cubs plodded hesitantly down a street dusted with newly fallen snow. She had been driven from choice waiting areas along the Hudson Bay shore toward Cape Merry by dominant bears. The sow sensed danger in the alien surroundings of town. But she also smelled food, which, despite the danger, was too much to resist. She stopped and sniffed in characteristic polar-bear fashion. Then one of the cubs let out a yowl.

As quickly as the sow investigated her cub's problem, human faces appeared in the yellow lights of doors and windows all around. The cub had stepped on one of the nail-driven plywood sheets commonly placed around Churchill homes as a defense and bear alarm. Somebody dialed the Polar Bear Alert number, and soon a team of trained men from the Department of Natural Resources arrived on the scene.

Within 24 hours, the sow bear had been captured in a culvert trap and the cubs shot with tranquilizing darts. The whole family was then released in what really amounts to a bear jail, or detention center. Their sentence was confinement until Hudson Bay froze over, which happened to be in just a few days.

The idea of a bear detention center originated in 1976 as one of several recommendations to the Manitoba government by a concerned citizens' advisory committee. The concept of holding bears for a short time to keep them out of trouble was remarkably simple.

Prior to the 1970s, a large Armed Forces base was located east of Churchill. When the base was phased out, many of the buildings were offered to the province of Manitoba. One large triple Quonset hut, designated by the Army and known to this day as D20, was selected for the bears. It could accommodate 20 separate "cells" constructed of cement blocks with barred steel doors. The first troublesome bears were incarcerated in 1982, and since then this seems to have been a successful project.

Jailed bears are not fed, but they are watered. The first bears trapped during the fall might have to endure confinement for a month or two, but most are held for weeks at the longest. When the

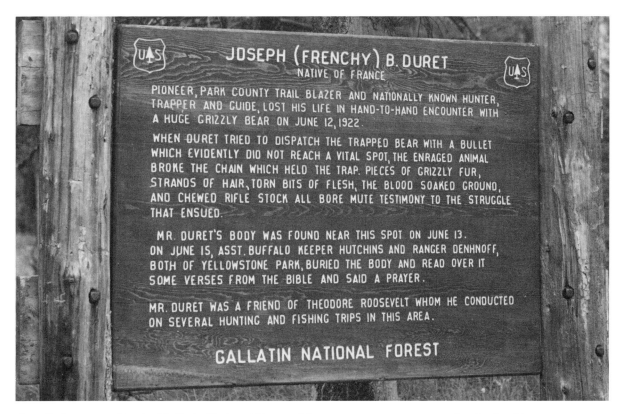

JOSEPH (FRENCHY) B. DURET
NATIVE OF FRANCE

PIONEER, PARK COUNTY TRAIL BLAZER AND NATIONALLY KNOWN HUNTER, TRAPPER AND GUIDE, LOST HIS LIFE IN HAND-TO-HAND ENCOUNTER WITH A HUGE GRIZZLY BEAR ON JUNE 12, 1922.

WHEN DURET TRIED TO DISPATCH THE TRAPPED BEAR WITH A BULLET WHICH EVIDENTLY DID NOT REACH A VITAL SPOT, THE ENRAGED ANIMAL BROKE THE CHAIN WHICH HELD THE TRAP. PIECES OF GRIZZLY FUR, STRANDS OF HAIR, TORN BITS OF FLESH, THE BLOOD SOAKED GROUND, AND CHEWED RIFLE STOCK ALL BORE MUTE TESTIMONY TO THE STRUGGLE THAT ENSUED.

MR. DURET'S BODY WAS FOUND NEAR THIS SPOT ON JUNE 13. ON JUNE 15, ASST. BUFFALO KEEPER HUTCHINS AND RANGER DENHNOFF, BOTH OF YELLOWSTONE PARK, BURIED THE BODY AND READ OVER IT SOME VERSES FROM THE BIBLE AND SAID A PRAYER.

MR. DURET WAS A FRIEND OF THEODORE ROOSEVELT WHOM HE CONDUCTED ON SEVERAL HUNTING AND FISHING TRIPS IN THIS AREA.

GALLATIN NATIONAL FOREST

A trail sign erected in the Gallatin National Forest, Montana, commemorates a classic, fatal bear encounter.

bears are eventually released onto frozen Hudson Bay, most scatter out onto the featureless ice without a backward glance.

There are several notable advantages to the detention idea. Foremost is that serious trouble has been greatly reduced and fewer bears have had to be killed in the interest of public safety. It is also cheaper to move and hold captured animals close to town than to transport them far away by helicopter. Although the effect of this incarceration on bears is still unknown, the bears do not seem to suffer from confinement. They don't eat much at that time of year anyway. The program certainly seems to be a step in the right direction for the conservation of the ice bruin. Unfortunately, not all wildlife problems are handled so well everywhere by local citizens committees.

Alaskan homesteaders keep bears from pillaging their food supplies by building caches, such as this old one, on stilts. Sheet metal is wrapped around the legs to prevent black bears from climbing. Such caches prevent a lot of trouble today.

BEAR ATTACKS AND CITIZEN ALARM

During early autumn of 1984, my desk was littered with newspaper clippings of the past summer's bear incidents. It seemed there were more of these incidents than during many previous summers. Not since the August night in 1967 when two young women were killed by grizzly bears in separate attacks in Glacier National Park were bears so prominently in the headlines. Many of those headlines were appropriately grisly. Consider some examples:

Blind Youth Looks Ahead: "An Auke Bay, Alaskan youth who was blinded and disfigured by a bear was in Boston today to undergo plastic surgery and to receive instructions on how to live in a world of darkness. Seven weeks ago the life of [the young man] was almost snuffed out. He was fishing with a friend when attacked by a bear. He fired one shot before the animal knocked him flat. The animal took the whole front of the man's face in its mouth, across the eyes from temple to temple, scraping the eyes with its teeth and leaving a trench across the man's face. Then the

But the park officials did not attempt to trap the bear, and by midsummer it had wandered away from the small settlement area.

By this time though, almost every hiking or fishing party to Trout Lake reported seeing a lean, thin-faced bear of unusual and aggressive behavior. It was the same one. I had hiked to Trout Lake two years before and recall that it was a potential magnet for a bear. People had caught trout, dressed the fish (leaving the entrails on the shore), and often cooked them on the spot. It was not a very neat area, and would have attracted scavenging animals. Again, park personnel should have been aware of this, as well as the numerous bear warnings, and they might have again removed the troublesome bruin.

When the bear was shot by two park rangers two days after it killed the girl, one of the two rangers believed the bear was actually stalking them where they had been sleeping in a small shelter cabin. There was no question about that particular bear being the culprit, because its stomach contained light brown hair of a Caucasian.

Hindsight is certainly better than foresight, but surely park authorities should also have anticipated the tragedy at Granite Chalet. All summer long, bears had been coming nightly to feed at an open garbage dump not far from the Chalet, an overnight accommodation for hikers. Although it was and is strictly against regulations to feed animals in such a manner, several members of the park staff had actually watched the nightly "show." If they reported the violation, no one of greater authority paid any attention. In fact the nightly appearance of bears had become a main attraction that summer of '67, and many tourists made the trek especially to watch it.

Because the Chalet was such a popular place, it was unable to furnish overnight facilities for all hikers on trails converging in the area. So the Park Service designated a small area as a public campground for backpackers only a short distance away. The main trouble was that it was poorly located, practically astride a main bear trail leading toward the Chalet garbage dump.

A young bear scavenging in a garbage dump is a too-frequent occurrence in bear country. Scavenging is a bad and unhealthy habit that will inevitably lead the animal to serious trouble with man.

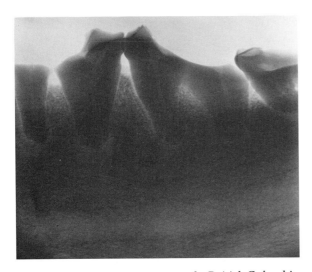

This is an X ray of the lower jaw of a British Columbia grizzly that attacked a human. Says Dr. Alice Richter of Jackson, Wyoming, "the marked wear of posterior teeth indicates an old animal. The crowns of the teeth were worn down to the nerve chambers, with abcesses occurring on all roots. The bear had to be surviving on a soft diet of berries and maybe fish." The condition of the teeth probably explains the bear's mean disposition.

On that terrible night, another bear dragged a second girl (also a seasonal park employee) from her sleeping bag and mauled her almost beyond recognition. She should never have been sleeping near an open garbage dump, which shouldn't have existed in the first place, or beside a busy bear pathway. Like the Trout Lake horror, this one might have been avoided just by applying common sense and enforcing a no-feeding regulation.

Immediately after the tragedy, park rangers baited the Granite dump and sat to wait for the killer bear to return. Altogether three bears came to the bait, and all three were shot. But not one of the three (all of which were females, one with two cubs, which escaped) bore any evidence whatever of being the "guilty" bear. The stomachs did not contain human remains, and no dried blood was found on the paws or muzzles.

Many bear maulings occur when bears are surprised by humans. For example, a bear may be feeding on a carcass, or guarding it, when all at once an unwary hiker approaches from downwind. The normal reaction is to drive the hiker away, which may mean more than just bluffing a charge. Or, the same wilderness traveler may

inadvertently come between a sow and a cub. The sow will also probably charge. But in most of these cases, the person attacked will emerge with only injuries and memories of terror. Bears simply guarding their "possessions" do not often kill people. The intention is only to drive them away.

Very old and/or sick bears present a more serious menace because they are unusually unpredictable. These are also bears that, in desperation, are more likely to turn to artificial sources of food—toward places frequented by careless humans. The more these bears haunt such places, the bolder they become.

Especially with grizzly bears, there is growing evidence that the live-trapping and handling techniques that have permitted us to scientifically study the species could also cause the bears to lose any natural fear of humans. One such case is worth describing.

Early in June 1984, a grizzly killed and ate a man in a public campground of the Gallatin National Forest, Montana, just west of Yellowstone National Park. The animal was quickly trapped nearby. It was killed and studied after officials determined positively that it was responsible for the man's death. Some interesting facts emerge from that study. First, the bear weighed 435 pounds when killed, which was far less than the 608 pounds it had weighed when live-trapped the previous fall just before hibernation. Probably that light weight was normal for the bear in early summer, following a long winter of semi-sleep.

But the most startling fact was that the bruin had been live-trapped a total of 19 times during its approximate 13-year existence. Ken Greer, laboratory supervisor of the Montana Department of Fish, Wildlife and Parks, was asked whether the 19 trappings could have caused the bear to lose all fear of humans. Greer said they would not, and eminent bear biologists have since agreed that the drugging and handling of themselves do not make bears more likely to lose fear of humans. But that is hard to accept without questions.

Records reveal that the bear was first captured when it was one year old, during a time when much effort was being made around Yellowstone Park to keep bears away from garbage. Old dumps were being fenced. The young grizzly was then transported from West Yellowstone on the edge of the park, where it had been caught, to well inside the park.

The future killer was again live-trapped in 1974, when it returned to West Yellowstone and tried to break into the fenced dump. The bear was transported again, this time farther away. Two years later it returned. During the next nine years the bear was in and out of traps almost continually and may even have set some sort of record for trapped grizzlies. Sometimes the bear was drugged and handled. Other times it was simply relocated to a distant spot. Like most typical bears, it had a seemingly infallible homing instinct.

Eight months before it attacked the man in the campground, the bear was trapped twice and relocated because it was prowling close to occupied cabins in the West Yellowstone area. One of these times the bear was moved to the Sunlight Basin area, 75 miles east of its home territory. Again, it quickly came back.

Biologist Greer could recall no instance when the bear had ever acted aggressively toward people, despite its long history of captures. Most wildlife enthusiasts who study bears of any kind experience their share of frightening moments, and those who observe grizzlies are likely to be treed at least once. Yet, a wildlife student who had been observing this bear, and had frequent meetings with it for several years, was never even threatened.

That West Yellowstone bear probably should have been destroyed. It certainly had an abnormal amount of contact with human beings throughout its life, though it had seemed to be more of a nuisance than a menace. Ken Greer remains as baffled as most other bear biologists who are familiar with the tragedy. "There is no clear reason for the attack," he has said, "nothing we can really hang our hat on."

Not all terrifying encounters with bears involve grizzlies. Black bears can also be very dangerous. Here is a letter from an Alaskan trapper that was published in *Alaska* magazine:

Yesterday, June 14, I was packing supplies to my cabin on Gold King Creek on the north

slope of the Alaska Range. At intervals the trail followed the edge of a bluff and it was fairly bushy except for the edge. It was raining lightly and the bugs were bothering me. Thus I was wet and pestered and under a heavy load, and not paying proper attention to the trail. I had no rifle as I was clearing limbs and such with a machete as I traveled. My dog Brute was following me.

I was suddenly aware of a large black bear coming at me from about eight feet away. There had been no sound of her coming. Her ears were back and she had her back humped up like a cat. In the next instant I hit her across the face with the machete. This turned her a few feet down the bluff where she turned and started back at me. Then the dog started barking and she made for him.

I managed to get the pack off and run about 50 feet to an aspen with about an eight-inch butt. I don't know how I managed to get to the top but I did, and with the machete still in hand. No sooner had I gotten up as far as I could when the bear hit the tree and climbed up and touched my boot with her nose, then fell back down and went for the dog again. In a matter of seconds she made another running climb after me. She hit the tree with such force I nearly fell out. This time I instinctively hit her again with the machete. Her nose was badly cut from the end to under the right eye. The second machete slash had cut her across her right eye and ear, and the eye was lying exposed on her cheek.

When she again fell to the ground and chased the dog I realized I was in real trouble. She had reached my feet on the second climb, and I could go no higher. I had one foot in a small crotch but knew that if she got a bite on it and fell back I would be dragged down.

After running the dog off the second time she came for me again. Again I hit her with the machete, this time right between the ears with all the force I could exert while bending down and holding on with one hand. She was bleeding and blowing blood up the tree. She still had made no sound other than the gurgling of blood.

After this third machete slash she fell back to the ground and rolled over and staggered again to her feet. She made another run at the dog with three or four *wuff wuffs*, then ran over the bluff. At this time I saw a small cub behind her.

I was not sure she wouldn't come back, so I stayed in the tree for perhaps 15 minutes. As

I smoked a cigarette and waited I noticed that the whole tree was trembling like a leaf in the wind. I had had no time for fear until after the encounter, which I don't believe lasted much over five minutes.

I had never experienced such fury. The bear had torn up a large area and shredded my tree in minutes. After my first slash at her with the machete she was berserk, and I know she would have killed me if I had been knocked out of the tree.

After the dog had circled around without further trouble I climbed out of the tree, thoroughly shaken. I retrieved my backpack, hat, and sunglasses that I had lost on the initial run, then cleared out of the area.

Today as I sit in my cabin nursing scrapes and bruises that I don't remember getting, I can reflect and be thankful for Brute who gave me the few seconds needed to get into the tree. I am convinced that his presence alone saved my

life—or at least saved me from a bad mauling. I also realize that even if I had been armed with a rifle there would have been no time at the first contact with the bear to use it. She would have hit me in the legs, and with the heavy pack I would have been upset and mauled when I hit the ground. Only the instinctive swat with the machete turned her.

I advise travelers to beware at this time of year. Bears are harassed by the bugs, and some have cubs and are very short-tempered. The new foliage makes it hard to see far ahead. Take along a dog—the added nose and eyes and presence may save your life.

I have encountered and observed many, many bears in my years in the Bush, but never before have I seen anything so swift and furious. I am trying to get hold of the Department of Fish and Game today to see if they can find her and make sure she is able to take care of the cub. Jim Smith, Trapper, Gold King Creek.

This is the skull of a brown bear that killed two and maimed two others on Admiralty Island, Alaska. The teeth are not in the best condition.

Even a large dog is no match for an angry adult black bear, but the same bear may try to flee from a pack of canine pursuers. It is a bad mistake to take a dog into grizzly areas "for protection."

ATTACK VICTIMS

It is interesting how often some people who are attacked by bears still retain a respect and even an affection for the animals. Trapper Jim Smith, in the previous account, was concerned about the black bear cub, possibly orphaned. Another man, Bob Wilkinson, who was mauled badly by a grizzly, sat up in his hospital bed and said, "I don't want to hear of any campaign to annihilate grizzlies because of this. The grizzly is the true monarch of the hills. He's so smart he makes me and the rest of us seem stupid."

Wilkinson, 41, a railway machinist and part-time hunting guide, was tracking elk when he encountered three grizzlies in the Bob Marshall Wilderness of northwestern Montana. Several years before, a grizzly had mauled a farmer to death in the same general area. The three bruins probably comprised a family, a sow with large twin yearling cubs. Two of them, probably the cubs, moved away when they saw Wilkinson, but the other turned. Weighing about 450 pounds, it hung its head to one side, *woofed*, and charged head-on.

"I've seen hundreds of bears," Wilkinson said, "but this was the first one to do anything but run away. So I ducked behind a tree and let the bear go by."

Wilkinson then started to climb the tree. But the trunk was so smooth and the hunter's boots so slick that when the bear came back, he was still only about 5 feet above ground. The bear grabbed a foot and tore off one boot. Wilkinson frantically kept climbing and then the other boot was ripped off. With both boots gone, he was able to get a better grip and kept climbing until he ran out of tree, which was only about 15 feet tall.

"I sat there in the treetop and looked down,

thinking I had her licked," Wilkinson recalls. "But she started up the trunk after me again. She grabbed one of my ankles and wrenched.

"We both fell, the grizzly all the way to the ground with part of my foot, and me about halfway. Hanging desperately in the tree, I thought it was the end. I knew the bear would return and finish me. But instead it lumbered away without once looking back."

CLOSE CALLS

Not all bear confrontations end in tragedy. In fact most, fortunately, leave only a chilling episode branded in the memory. So we will end the gruesome tales here with a story that is more typical.

Late in August 1984, Peggy and I had been photographing grizzlies and other wildlife in Denali National Park. Because Denali is one of the great wildlife repositories on earth, it is no wonder that many wildlife photographers congregate here late every summer. Among them was our friend, Tom Mangelson, of Jackson, Wyoming, taking a busman's holiday after filming his fine television documentary on whooping cranes for the National Geographic Society.

The campgrounds in Denali are primitive, and the weather was unseasonably warm, so Mangelson decided to take a bath in Igloo Creek. He stripped down and winced as he waded into the icy water. Then he turned around and stood, naked and nearly frozen, facing a grizzly bear. Without looking directly at Mangelson, the bear ate his bar of biodegradable soap, sniffed his clothes, and disappeared into dense alders. So much for keeping clean.

HUNTING AND ART

Although I regard our native bears first and foremost as irreplaceable symbols of the wilderness, they have other important values to other people. Black bears are abundant enough in many places to be hunted for sport and for bear rugs, which makes them economically valuable. Many communities across America depend on hunting as a regular source of income. A substantial percentage of all hunting and camping equipment

manufactured is sold to bear hunters.

Since the beginning of recorded history, artisans have painted and sculpted the bears that shared their existence. Modern wildlife painters and sculptors are still busy depicting bears.

BEAR WATCHING AND PHOTOGRAPHY

Equally important is the fast-growing sport of wildlife watching and wildlife photography. Few creatures are more compelling than bears to watch and photograph in the wild. A lot of the tourists who travel north to Alaska and Denali National Park do so because it is by far the best (and in a way the last) place to be guaranteed grizzly-bear sightings. Once Yellowstone was in this category, but today visitors are lucky to spot a single bruin there, even at long range.

There are a number of wilderness camps in Canada and Alaska where one can safely view and film grizzlies or brown bears at moderately close camera range. Afognak Wilderness Lodge (Seal Bay via Kodiak, AK 99697) operated by Roy and Shannon Randall on Afognak Island, is one. Chenik Brown Bear Camp (Box 1557, Homer, AK 99603), operated by Kevin and Cindy

Modern American wildlife artists still feature bears in their work. Premier American sculptor Bob Scriver of Browning, Montana, creates grizzly bears in bronze.

Polar bears have always figured in Eskimo legend, culture, and art. Three soapstone carvings are typical of the best Eskimo bear carvings. (Courtesy of Winnipeg Art Gallery)

Sidelinger on the Alaska Peninsula about 15 miles from the McNeil River, is another. By far the best place we have ever found for watching inland grizzlies is Oldsquaw Lodge, Bag Service 2711, Whitehorse, Yukon, Canada Y1A 4K8. located along the long-abandoned Canol (oil pipeline) Road, east of Whitehorse on the Yukon-Northwest Territory border. It is operated by Sam Miller and Nan Eagleson. Miller is a veteran bear biologist and an outstanding field naturalist whose work I described earlier.

BEARS AND THE FUTURE

Many believe that bears—particularly griz-zlies—are not compatible with people, even in national parks, and that they should be eliminated. Perhaps in the long run, as the proliferating human population becomes even more of a cancer on the globe and the last wilderness is consumed, bears will indeed cease to exist. But I believe that we can still live with bears for a long time to come, if we regard them exactly as what they are: magnificent wild animals.

People interested in seeing and photographing bears can choose from a number of wilderness lodges. Oldsquaw Lodge on the Yukon-Northwest Territory border in Canada is among the best of these. Grizzlies are often spotted from the main lodge building.

CHAPTER 7

CONSERVATION AND THE FUTURE

A tranquilized grizzly is being fitted with permanent identification in Yellowstone Park. The bear shown is helpless, but is aware of what is taking place. Modern drugs instead render the bears unconscious and unaware of the human activity.

Men have been trapping bears by many different means for centuries. But it wasn't until 1952 that serious thought was given to trapping bears *alive* for scientific purposes and then releasing them. Until then, efforts to obtain bear information were handicapped by the lack of adequate techniques to capture and handle animals larger than men, and much, much stronger.

Starting practically from scratch, a young biologist, Albert Erickson, began to solve the trapping challenges at the Michigan Department of Conservation's Cusino Wildlife Experiment Station on the state's Upper Peninsula. Working in Alger and Schoolcraft Counties, Erickson managed to capture one bruin in 1952 and four in 1953. Stepping up his efforts in the summers, he trapped 43 bears in 1955 and 48 bears in 1956.

During the four-year project, 96 animals were handled a total of 109 times. Altogether it was immensely important pioneer work in the bear research field. Since then, biologists of 20 or more states have captured thousands of black bears using essentially the same techniques. As a result, scientists have produced quite a store of knowledge about a remarkable animal.

Erickson caught his bears in two basic types of traps: culvert, and steel-spring. The most successful culvert traps (which remain more or less standard to this day) were similar to those in use by the National Park Service to entrap nuisance bears.

Here biologists locate, bait, and set a standard culvert-type bear trap in Yellowstone National Park.

They were constructed of 8-foot sections of 36-inch corrugated steel culvert, and they were fitted with sheet metal drop doors at the front and open metal grids at the back. The culverts could be mounted on a bare trailer frame for quick and easy transport anywhere a vehicle can go, although in the beginning Erickson did not do so. Steel-spring wolf traps proved more successful and economical for catching bears than culvert traps. But the chances of injury to the bruins was greater with wolf traps and those traps made handling the bears more difficult. The heaviest bear secured in a steel-spring trap weighed 257 pounds. Heavier, stronger bears managed to escape the metal jaws. An unexpected problem was that people shot black bears they happened to find in the steel traps.

Live-trapping sites were selected by searching old logging trails for areas that had the most bear sign, including fresh tracks, scats, mauled stumps and logs, and limbs broken from trees and shrubs. On improved roads, Erickson and his crewmen dragged an 8-foot section of railroad iron or a conifer treetop behind their vehicle to obliterate old marks and help them find fresh sign on sub-

sequent days. Apple orchards and garbage dumps were also good areas to place traps.

The study soon showed that natural feeding areas varied with the season. In spring, the semi-open forest glades composed of lush grasses, strawberries, and pioneer shrub species seemed to attract the most bears. Summer was a good period to find them near abandoned homesteads and lumber camps, which were common throughout the northern Michigan bush, and which commonly held an abundance of fruiting plants. In autumn, Erickson learned to search wherever there was a good crop of black cherries as well as around overgrown and long-forgotten apple orchards. The reseachers tried to keep traplines short and to confine a series of bear traps to a single township at once. This saved travel time and also prevented injury and stress to the animals.

Culvert traps worked best when they were placed in the cool shade and well stabilized in a firm position, with dirt spread on the trap floor and in front of the trap. The dirt seemed to lessen an approaching animal's fear of the trap, possibly because it felt more natural underfoot than did bare metal. The loose earth also revealed whether or not a bear had come near or partially entered the trap. Learning the proper techniques for setting the bear traps also revealed much about a black bear's behavior.

The most consistently successful bait used for the Michigan black bears was fresh venison collected as roadkills. Pits around steel traps baited with fish and offal were visited and sometimes wallowed in, though the bait was seldom eaten. Table garbage was usually effective, as were anise-based scents.

Surprisingly, Erickson had minor or negligible success with apples, peanut butter, molasses, or sorghum. Although black bears will suffer terrible stinging to rob a wild beehive, there was only mild response when honey was used as a lure during this study.

Contrary to popular belief and even to what other biologists and hunting outfitters have reported, Al Erickson found that the bears showed a distinct aversion to eating putrid flesh. When his baits became fetid or heavily infested with maggots, they were no longer effective. During warm weather, it became necessary to rebait traps every few days to assure results. As summer progressed, the animals became more difficult to capture and were tempted by only the choicest offerings—no doubt because of the increasing bounty of natural foods. Black bears were easiest to trap early in May and June.

The bait average black bears could least resist was a chunk of venison of 10 pounds or more. Such a large bait also allowed a more secure attachment to the trigger wire. The trapping crew set trigger mechanisms to release when a pull of 25 to 40 pounds was applied. This eliminated the chance that small animals such as foxes could set the traps off.

Erickson and subsequent researchers soon learned that bears are not content to eat a bait or a dead animal where they find it. This is true of all North American bruins. They will at least try to move it and are usually successful. Thus when using the steel-spring traps, it was always necessary to stake the bait in place.

Once in a steel trap, the bear was handled by first slipping a choker over its head and around its neck and then by securely tying the legs with heavy rope. The choker consisted of pliable chain

loop fastened to the end of a 6-foot section of pipe held by a T-handle.

Handling an angry or confused bruin was dangerous business until a proper procedure could be worked out. Even then, it was no picnic. When approached, bears tended to back away to the limit of their trap chain. Handling-crew members soon learned that it was best to approach a bear simultaneously from several directions, acting calmly and making no sudden moves. That tactic often resulted in a bear standing quietly and not lunging in any one direction. It also reduced injury to paws, as well as the chance of pulling free of the trap. And the surround approach made it easier to slip the choker collar over the bear's head.

Getting the choker around the bear's neck on the first attempt was important, because it became very difficult after that. The noose was twisted until it was just tight enough to hold the bear. If the noose was tightened too much and breathing obstructed, even a fairly docile animal would turn violent. With the choker secured, one man could control the animal's head. Another crew member then grasped a rear leg, fastened a rope to it, and lashed the rope onto a solid object such as a tree. Unless that leg was also secured on the first attempt, the animal would grimly hold its legs under its body and out of reach. The end goal of the handling crew was to flip the bear onto its back, all legs roped, so that it could be anesthetized or tranquilized.

TRANQUILIZING AND HANDLING BEARS

In the pioneer days of live-trapping, anesthetizing was done with an ether cone slipped over the nose. Since then, it has been done with various other drugs easier to administer in the wild. When Erickson and his helper found a black bear trapped in a culvert, they sealed off all openings and made the culvert an anesthetizing chamber into which they pumped ether. But they were never really certain whether the "patient" was sufficiently unconscious. For one thing, the ether fumes prohibited close observation. More than once a bear had to be given artificial respiration because the dose of ether was too great. Just as often the shock of ear tagging or toe clipping resulted in a too-quick recovery. Two bears died of drug overdoses, ten suffered broken bones (including shattered jaws) and one was strangled. Thanks to newer and better drugs, trapped bears are now tranquilized with a syringe fastened on the end of a pole. That isn't nearly as exciting for the biologists as the old method, but none we've met miss that kind of excitement.

When a bear is tranquilized, it is marked for future identification by clamping numbered tags onto the ears, by tattooing the lips, or both. Blood samples may be taken. The bear's sex and the exact location of the trapping are noted. The animal is weighed and measured, and its general condition is noted. If the bear happens to be one considered a nuisance, a large number may be painted on its sides so that it can be easily identified from a distance by anyone. But painted numbers will last only until a bear's next shedding. Black bears also form a growth layer in the roots of their teeth each year. Thus, a small premolar is pulled, and the animal's age can be accurately determined by counting the dental layers just as a forester counts the growth rings of a tree. Normally an hour is necessary to gather all the information, after which the bear is moved to the coolest, shadiest spot nearby to sleep off the effect of the drugs.

Handling black bears apparently does not bother the animals too much. During the summer of 1976, Wisconsin biologists Bruce Kohn and Ned Norton live-captured 75 bears a total of 151 times in only 75 nights of trapping. That amounted to an average of over two bears every 24 hours, all in Iron County. Many bears were taken more than once. One, despite efforts to discourage it, was captured eight times. The bear either had a very poor memory or just didn't mind being jabbed with a syringe.

It is easy to understand how an inexperienced person who sees a black bear may regard it in the same way he would a large dog. Smokey the Forest Service bear, and Yogi the Disney bear, have advanced the image of bruins as either a truc human friend or a clown. Of course bears are neither of those. Adult bears are more powerful than the strongest men, as Kohn and Norton found out. Most of the traps used in their project were made from two standard 55-gallon barrels

arc-welded end to end, with the usual trip mechanism and trap door. Still, two bears escaped from the barrel traps by chewing and tearing their way through the metal. Two others had their heads free when the handling crew arrived. If you think black bears are not agile, consider that one 303-pound Wisconsin male managed to swap ends *inside* the barrel. A 396-pounder, the largest captured during the study, squeezed inside the trap just far enough to reach the bait and slam the door on its behind.

Nor are cubs the cute, cuddly little fellows they appear to be. Grab a wild one (while its mother sits inside a trap) and you might as well have a brawling, scratching, outraged bobcat on your hands. There is no place to clutch a bear cub where it can't grab you. From experience, biologists have learned that the way to handle a black-bear cub is to first chase it into a tree. Next, sedate it by means of a syringe on a pole. When the cub is immobilized, catch it in a net.

Charles Jonkel, who has studied black bears since the 1950s as a University of Montana researcher, handled about 600 individuals. Many of the bears were fitted with radio collars to trace their travels. Like Albert Erickson, Jonkel concluded that black-bears are not inherently mean or aggressive, but certainly can be. He told me once that most black-bear "attacks" were bluffs and that the way to deal with a bluffer was to run, yelling, directly toward it. Jonkel also believed that some bruins went into traps intentionally to freeload a meal, and then sat, bored, until the bear-handling crew came along to release them.

THE ROGERS STUDIES

Without doubt the longest ongoing black bear investigation has taken place in northern Minnesota. There U.S. Forest Service biologist Dr. Lynn Rogers has hoped to learn enough about bears of the region to influence forestry and timber-cutting practices more in favor of bears (and, incidentally, other wildlife). For example, he has identified exactly what bears in his study area eat and what their habitat requirements are. He has been able to compare breeding success of black bears in areas with different histories of

Live-trapping bears—in this case, black bears—was pioneered by biologist Albert Erickson in Michigan. Many of his early techniques are still used across the country.

forest fires and logging practices.

Beginning in 1969, Lynn Rogers has captured and released more than 1,000 bears. Altogether that represents a lot of hard physical work, chance-taking, scratches, jolts and bruises, and long cold or sweaty hours in the field. It also represents a life of adventure few can experience, as well as an unmatched knowledge of black bears.

Unlike most other biologists who have con-centrated solely on live-trapping bears, Rogers has specialized in study around winter dens. Dur-ing summer and fall trapping, Rogers fits certain key bears with radios. In March, he radio-tracks his way to wherever the animals are sleeping. The ticklish part begins when Rogers crawls on hands and knees into the occupied den.

Some bruins in dens sleep soundly, others more fitfully, depending on their metabolism. Some are so "slowed down" when the biologist enters that they barely raise their head. Rogers has been able to lay his head on the chest of some bears and listen to the heart before drugging them. But the next bear may suddenly awaken and stare un-certainly at the intruder.

In the den, Rogers wisely tries to make no sudden or startling moves. Instead he carefully tranquilizes the hibernating bears with a syringe on the end of a jab stick. With the drug admin-istered, Rogers retreats outside and waits 10 min-utes or so for the drug to take effect. The helpless animal, along with any cubs, is then dragged outside the den and placed on its back, legs splayed, for examination. There may be a ner-vous instant or two when the dazed bruin appears not to be drugged and makes an effort to revive. But because of the precise dosage of the drug, the bear is helpless for a while.

Rogers takes blood samples and checks for parasites. The blood will later be analyzed in Minneapolis for phosphorus, calcium, protein, glucose, blood urea, nitrogen, testosterone, and red and white blood cells. The blood test gives a good picture of the animal's overall health. The bear is also weighed on a balance beam. The bear's old radio collar, the one that led Rogers to the den, is replaced with a new one to avoid malfunction during the coming year. Any yearling cubs, spending their last winter with mother, are also collared. Then all are dragged back into the den and arranged in their original positions. It is hoped they will awaken feeling entirely natural and unmolested.

By the winter of 1983-84, Lynn Rogers had crawled into more than 200 musty black bear dens. He has collared a total of over 100 bears—practically every bear in his 100-square-mile study area. This type of investigation has given him a familiarity with the species that would be impossible any other way.

RESEARCH MONEY

Many people believe that money spent on bear research—or on anything environmental for that matter—is money wasted. You've seen one black bear and you've seen them all, or so the reasoning goes. A special venom seems to be reserved for people who are interested in working with bears to save them. In the May 3, 1984 issue of Wyoming's *Jackson Hole Guide*, a reader wrote (in part) to the editor: "I think we should make radio collars out of the biologists' tranquilizing guns and wrap them around their necks. That way we can keep track of the biologists."

Especially in Alaska, the battle lines have been clearly drawn over whether it is worth spending tax dollars on programs to save the grizzly. One controversial program of May 1979 involved the transporting of 47 grizzlies from an area north of the Denali Highway to protect spring moose calves.

While observing wolves, biologists of the Alaska Department of Fish and Game made the incidental discovery that bears were killing a significant number of newly born moose calves. Thus, the 47 bears were airlifted and or trucked as far as 200 miles away. The biologists realized that some of the bears would return to the region where they were trapped; still, the scientists hoped to give the calves some respite during their highly vulnerable first six weeks of life. The biologists were genuinely surprised at how quickly the trapped grizzlies filtered back into their home habitat. Many were back in less than a month's time.

That mass relocation of almost 12 tons of live bear was probably the largest such animal transfer ever attempted. Although it may have failed in one sense, it furnished still more evidence of a bear's homing instinct—of its astonishing ability to travel far across unfamiliar wilderness to reach familiar haunts. Scientists still don't know how this is possible.

YELLOWSTONE AND THE CRAIGHEAD POSITION

Unfortunately, what we have learned about bears has not always been applied to their conservation. Take the case of Yellowstone, the world's first national park and one of the most splendid wilderness areas on earth. Along with Glacier National Park, it is one of the two final inviolate sanctuaries for grizzly bears in the United States, south of Alaska.

"Bears in the Yellowstone," an early visitor wrote around the turn of the 20th century, "are as the autumn leaves; plentiful." Ever since its declaration as a park by President Grant in 1872, Yellowstone has been synonymous with bears. For generations, people have traveled to Yellowstone to see bears more than they have to see any of the other natural wonders. The animal they saw, mainly, was the black bear, which was regarded as an appealing though slightly dangerous clown that freeloaded food along park highways and sometimes also prowled the campgrounds. The "bear jams" created when people paused to watch and photograph seemingly tame black bears sometimes blocked traffic for miles. I have talked to many people who remembered their Yellowstone bear encounters longer and with more warmth than any other events during a lifetime of summer holidays. Some of them still come back to Yellowstone hoping to see the bears.

Not many Yellowstone visitors ever saw a grizzly, though. Grizzlies did not often panhandle on the roads and largely avoided campgrounds.

This once-familiar sight of a black bear panhandling from a passing car in Yellowstone Park is mostly a thing of the past. The roadside bears have been virtually eliminated.

But they were there. And you *could* see grizzlies if you scanned the landscape carefully in the late spring and early summer before most tourists arrived. Once toward the end of May, I counted 11 grizzlies in one day. Yet in the past 12 years, I have seen only 13 bears altogether. No two authorities agree on how many are left in Yellowstone today, but it is a pitiful few, surely fewer than 200 and possibly less than 150. Of these, only about 30 are in the critically important category of mature females.

When visitors enter Yellowstone today, they are meticulously reminded of the bears they are unlikely to see. Signs at all park entrances warn that bears and other large animals are dangerous, and that they should be viewed from a safe distance. Folders on how to behave in bear country are handed to all travelers when they pay the admission fee. There are bear warning signs in all campgrounds, in toilets, and even stenciled on wooden campground tables. Park officials have become almost paranoid over bears, and not entirely without reason. In 1972, for example, an Alabama man was killed by a bear. Although the man had been camping illegally in a closed area, a judge ruled the Park Service had been negligent about warning the man of bear danger and awarded his family $87,000. Other bear problems since then have made park authorities extremely cautious. To many, they may seem overly cautious because no bears are anywhere in sight.

So where have all the bears gone?

Ask a ranger in a visitor center, and the ranger will say that they are "in the backcountry where they belong," or that the bruins have "gone wild." They are present, we are assured, but just out of sight. In 1984, a ranger assured me that the lack of sightings was a result of the park's policy over the past dozen years of weaning bears from dependence on human food. The ranger further stated that the program had been quite successful, and that now truly wild bruins were afraid of man, living in the backcountry.

Sadly there is little truth in any of this. Griz-

These culvert-trap photos were made during the Craighead brothers' grizzly-bear study, along Trout Creek. The studies revealed more about grizzlies than all research before and since.

zlies, and blacks as well, have not so much gone wild as they have mostly been killed.

From the late 1800s until the 1960s, foraging around park garbage dumps was a way of life for Yellowstone grizzlies. For a while, some feeding was done in a designated area for public viewing near Old Faithful. But beginning in 1969, the major garbage dumps in the park were suddenly closed with a fairly high bear population and a new park policy aimed at "restoring natural balances." A decade and a half later, with roughly a 50 percent drop in the grizzly population since the dump closing, feeding bears has again been proposed as a way to save the animals. It is a controversial approach, but is certainly worth consideration.

Earlier I described briefly some of the scientific work of John and Frank Craighead with Yellowstone grizzlies. From 1959 until 1971 the biologists amassed what is perhaps the bulk of everything known about grizzlies to this day. The Craigheads contended that the Yellowstone Park dumps not only supplemented the nutrition of grizzly bears, but kept them concentrated and safe within park boundaries during the summer. The Craigheads did not actually oppose closing the dumps, but they did strongly recommend doing so gradually. Frank Craighead explained to me that bears feeding at the dump on Trout Creek were similar to brown bears visiting a salmon stream every summer to feed on fish. The bruins had come to depend on the dump as a reliable source of food. Frank was convinced that closing the dumps abruptly would cause serious problems for both the bears and man.

But the dumps were abruptly closed anyway by order of park superintendent Jack Anderson in 1971, at the same time Anderson terminated the Craigheads unfinished study within Yellowstone. Anderson ordered the Craighead laboratory bulldozed to the ground. Radio collars were removed from all bears as being unsightly. Anderson was also the man who first permitted snowmobilers in the previously quiet, exquisite park.

As the Craigheads had predicted, the following years were hectic. Scores of bears had to be killed both inside and beyond the park. Others that did not have to be killed were eliminated anyway to be on the safe side. Says former park naturalist and Yellowstone Park historian Paul Schullery: "Policies toward the grizzly changed dramatically at this time. Any bear sighted in an area where it could come into contact with people was actively dealt with in some way."

Many of the bears killed by park rangers had raided campsites because they were deprived of the dumps. Unaccustomed hunger made them mean and aggressive. Some of those bears avoided campsites, but were killed as nuisances outside the park. John Craighead estimated that 2.5 times as many bears were killed outside the park during the ten years of dump closure as during the previous decade. Much of the bear "control work" was done by inexperienced personnel unqualified to handle bears, so that many bears were simply killed by accident or negligence. Yellowstone officials occasionally reported on how many bears were removed, but there was little truth to those reports. Bears killed accidentally were never reported at all. The Craigheads estimated that during the first five years after dump closure, 150 bears had been eliminated because the best available scientific data was ignored. That figure may have been on the conservative side. The bottom line is that the Yellowstone grizzly population is declining and their future is generally bleak.

An Interagency Grizzly Bear Committee was organized in an attempt to stop the decline of Yellowstone grizzlies. It is a task force of both federal and state bear people responsible for monitoring grizzly bear welfare and populations, and for making management recommendations. Many of the most qualified bear biologists, including John Craighead, are Committee members. Not all the members agree on the best ways to save the grizzlies of the Yellowstone area. They do not agree, for example, on whether supplemental feeding should be undertaken as an emergency measure.

For years Frank Craighead has strongly recommended supplemental feeding, perhaps in some dump kind of situation. He points out that during his and his brother's studies in the 1960s, the average litter size of grizzlies was 2.2 cubs. But for the period from 1975 until 1982, the Interagency Commission determined that the average litter size was only 1.9 cubs. Even a small drop in the reproductive rate is significant in a species with a reproduction rate as low as the grizzly's. Thus there is the theory that the grizzlies' reproduction rate was lowered by a loss of nutrition caused by closing the dumps. Such diverse organizations as the Wyoming Audubon Society and the Wyoming Outfitters Association agree with Frank Craighead that supplemental feeding may reverse the trend toward lowered reproduction.

The most commonly suggested method of supplemental feeding is to shoot the surplus elk and bison of certain Yellowstone areas. The populations of both species are very high; in fact the number of bison is rapidly getting out of hand. Buffalo have begun to wander outside Yellowstone boundaries to places where they threaten to become a greater nuisance than the bears. They may also be degrading some ranges.

As yet, officials do not recommend a supplemental feeding program. They cite the excessive cost, repercussions from the public, and dubious benefits as the reasons. But they have not ruled out feeding in specific instances as a management tool. If a certain bear takes to killing sheep outside the park, for example, a manager might be able to shoot an elk or a buffalo to distract it until the sheep can be moved elsewhere. The trouble is that sheep herders shoot grizzlies as soon as they see them.

Official disapproval of feeding is also based on a shaky assumption that annual bear mortality can be kept low or reduced. In other words, officials would strive to reduce poaching, accidental shooting, and killing of nuisance bears around campgrounds and livestock herds. Removing human pressure, such as continued resort developments, timber cutting, and mineral exploration in grizzly habitat, would certainly help. Eliminating livestock-grazing in critical areas near or adjacent to the park would be a splendid place to start. Summed up, something must be done, and soon.

Says John Craighead: "We knew enough about Yellowstone Grizzlies to save them in 1971. We ought to start using that information before we have counted the last one."

Supplemental feeding is not likely to become firm policy unless there is great public and conservationist demand for it soon. Unfortunately, feeding the bears would be to admit that official public policy over the past 15 years was a mistake that only succeeded in sacrificing most of the animals. The greatest objection to feeding is often more philosophical than scientific. According to Mary Meagher, a resource management specialist in Yellowstone, feeding bears is unthinkable. She is quoted as saying on the subject, "We cannot play God." That sentiment, while perhaps well-meant, is sadly out of place when dealing with the survival of a magnificent species. It is like saying that it is perfectly all right to trap and remove, or even to kill, a bear that threatens harm around a campground, but that it is wrong to feed the same bear to keep it away from trouble.

Strangely, park officials did not see it as playing God when they wisely removed a sow with three cubs living on Frank Island in Yellowstone Lake. The cubs were so undernourished that one even died during the transfer.

Because it is not endangered elsewhere, the decline of the black bear in Yellowstone has drawn less attention than the decline of the grizzly, even though it may be even more serious. Two different park spokesmen assured me that there were about 500 to 600 black bears in the park in 1984 (all, of course, living wild in the backcountry). The fact is, there are few black bears living anywhere in Yellowstone. During the 1970s, black bears were being terminated wholesale right along with grizzlies. The species has never really recovered. The simple, unalterable fact is that we can never guarantee the survival of bears, or much other wildlife, unless there is sufficient suitable habitat to sustain them. And we must not kill more than can be replaced each year.

THE ALASKAN BEAR PICTURE

The grizzly and brown bear situation in Alaska is much brighter than in Yellowstone, but it still warrants watching. Browns and grizzlies are probably as abundant in the 49th state today as they were half a century ago. State biologists estimate that 15,000 animals still stalk the state. Sound game management and sensible hunting regulations have usually been the rule in Alaska. The annual legal harvest of brown and grizzly bears runs about 730 animals, though the mortality from all causes may be twice that. More than any other factor, the large bear population is possible only because Alaska is so vast— completely "without limits," as so many old-time Alaskans like to think.

But Alaska may be coming to a crossroads. It is one of the fastest-growing states in the nation, and the human population is inexorably spreading into bear country. Most of the new people flooding the state come to Alaska because of the extraordinary outdoor opportunities, as well as for a fresh start in what is absolutely the last frontier. Thus, more and more people will be coming into conflict with bears. And the bears will probably be the losers.

During a recent visit to Alaska, my friend— well-known writer, photographer, and guide— Tom Walker mentioned some troublesome areas of concern. He described how great numbers of bruins became addicted to living around construction camps and garbage dumps during construction of the Alaska pipeline. An unrecorded but substantial number of grizzlies were dispatched between Prudhoe and Valdez, and the evidence was covered up by bulldozers.

Walker also reports that minor bear attacks and maulings have been on the increase as more and more people build cabins and try to carve a living on the fringes of civilization. These attacks have generated widespread fear in some areas, and the fear can lead to paranoia. According to Walker, in 1981 at the edge of a remote community, a resident was mauled by a female grizzly protecting her cubs. As serious and terrible as bear attacks may be, sows attacking to protect cubs rarely kill people. They seem to be trying to gain time for cubs to escape. During the next month or so, however, 18 bears were found shot to death in the area. It wouldn't take many such incidents to deplete a bear population.

Another confrontation between brown bears and cattle raisers has been festering for a long time in an unlikely place, Kodiak Island (where cattle raising should never have begun in the first

Next page: This grizzly mother with cub is a splendid example of the species in Yellowstone, where the animals were once seen often by travelers.

place). Some lands should belong just to bears. Kodiak, where the largest bruins on earth are born, is foremost of those lands.

Older Alaskan conservationists still cringe when they recall the times around 1960 when aircraft with machine guns were used to shoot bears that were killing cattle only recently introduced. Most of the bruins live on the Kodiak National Wildlife Refuge, but occasionally some do venture northward beyond refuge boundaries onto lands where the livestock represents an easy chunk of protein. The Kodiak Stock Grower's Association has complained that bear predation is on the increase, which revives fears of airplanes and machine guns. Wouldn't it be such a worthwhile project for the federal government to acquire all of the so-called cattle lands on Kodiak and add these to the Kodiak National Wildlife Refuge?

Legitimate, fair-chase hunting does not threaten Alaska's bears, but illegal hunting by hoodlum guides does have authorities worried. Poaching threatens to become big business. A prime brown hide, delivered to a client, goes for as high as $10,000. Alaska, where a light bush plane is almost as common as a pickup, is an ideal land for hunting from the air, which is completely outside the law.

To give some idea of the dimensions of bear and other big-game poaching, in 1981 Alaskan wildlife wardens broke up a ring of outfitters and guides, some unlicensed, who had killed 39 bears in two weeks' time. Their incentive for this criminal activity was estimated at $250,000 in trophy and "guide" fees. An increasing amount of the illegal traffic in big-game trophies is between Alaska and Europe. Rich European hunters seem suddenly desperate for Alaskan bear rugs and caribou antlers.

Still another matter haunts the future of Alaska's bears. Under the 1972 Alaska Native Claims Act passed by the U.S. Congress, 40 million acres of land have passed or is passing into the private ownership of Aleuts, Indians, and Eskimos. Only time will reveal how this will actually change the land, but it is not likely to be for the better. If conservationists, hunters, and wildlife biologists are not alarmed, they should be. There is every indication that bears and other wildlife will be given no consideration whatsoever, unless they can be turned to a quick profit. Native ownership of once-uninhabited, prime wildlife habitat is bound to produce more bear-man conflict.

It would be easy to fill a library with incidents that concern the future of bears in North America. The following account has a more favorable ending than most.

POISONING

During the early 1980s, the normally high population of moose had been dwindling in a somewhat remote region of northern Saskatchewan. It was believed that black bears were responsible for the decline because they preyed on moose calves. Although some studies have indicated that this has been true elsewhere in Canada, no research was done in the affected area of northern Saskatchewan. Nevertheless, a plan was devised to kill at least half of the area's estimated 50 black bears.

Rangers hung out 50 baits over a wide area of forest and scrub land favored by both the bruins and moose. The baits were peeled beaver carcasses and plastic containers of lard, both laced with strychnine. Death from strychnine poisoning is not always swift and never painless. The baits were monitored by helicopter.

But the planned month-long poisoning campaign was halted half-way through for two reasons: public outcry, and the fact that it was an expensive failure. The biologists in choppers could find only two bears that had taken the poison, although others might have escaped to die beyond detection. It is also likely that there were far fewer bears in the area to begin with—and that what was possibly an abnormally large moose population was only fluctuating back to a more normal level. The indiscriminate use of poison outraged everyone from local trappers to conservationists as far away as Ottawa and Vancouver. The question still remains: How many small mammals and birds were wiped out by the poison meant for bears?

With hunting regulations in force, the polar bear's chief threats include habitat incursions by man and chemical contamination of the oceans.

Peggy here wears knee-high boots and works with backpack on, ready to move with the action.

getting into position for a good shot would be as hard as approaching an old whitetail buck that has survived many hunting seasons.

The alternative is to photograph bears in parks and sanctuaries where most of them might survive to a ripe old age. These refuge bears are still as wild and unpredictable as any others; the difference is that they have come to trust human beings enough to occasionally allow them within camera range. In a few places, bruins allow people to approach quite close.

BEAR SAVVY

Regardless of the place, camera-hunting success depends on the photographer's knowing something about bears, about their habits and reactions. It is important to recognize bear sign and good bear habitat. Timing is also important, although not quite as critical as when shooting deer. We have found bears to be most active early and late in the day; yet the animals may be just as visible during the middle of the day, especially from late summer onward.

As in all photography, better and better results come with more and more experience. In time, a photographer is able to interpret bear body-language and predict what an individual animal is going to do next. Success also depends on the patience of the photographer. A lucky person might be able to shoot roll after roll of great bear pictures his first day out. But more than likely he will have to devote plenty of time to the fascinating game before shooting a photo trophy. Beside having the proper equipment (which I'll discuss) and ample patience, success has often depended on a handy supply of insect repellent, a foul weather suit or insulated parka, and good binoculars or a spotting scope. Few bears pose in warm sunlight on windless slopes. Some of the most terrible mosquitos we have ever met swarmed on the edge of the same swamp where we were shooting a Michigan black bear. Bitterly cold winds have blown over the same tundra ridges where we huddled waiting for a grizzly to stroll into range.

APPROACHING BEARS

We never try to actually stalk bears from downwind, remaining unseen and unheard as a gun-hunter might do. Nor do we advocate that any reader try it. We never try to approach any bruin as closely as, say, a deer or moose. To keep a

232

safe distance, we rely on longer telephoto lenses than we normally prefer. All this may seem overly cautious to some who are unfamiliar with wild bruins, but there simply is no point in taking unnecessary chances. Every bruin—in fact every creature from chipmunk to caribou—has an invisible and changing limit of tolerance. Go beyond that limit and a bear will either hurry away or charge you. Neither reaction is to a photographer's advantage.

The best advice when filming bears is always to stay within their sight, hearing, and scent, never making sudden or startling moves. If you try to sneak up on a grizzly, you may be suddenly discovered and in deep trouble. But approaching slowly, obliquely, never directly toward the animal, is good common sense. The fact that a bear does not look up directly at you does not mean that you are not under surveillance. If the bear is grazing as you begin an approach, it will probably continue to graze until its tolerance limit is approached. The moment the bear suddenly stops is usually the moment for you to stop, too.

BAITING AND BLINDS

It is quite possible to photograph bears from blinds, over bait, as gun-hunters often do, because few bears can resist enticing food. But this must not be undertaken lightly. Never, absolutely never, place any bait anywhere in the vicinity of dwellings, camps, or other places frequented by people. That only encourages a bear to go into an area in which it does not belong, thereby dooming the animal and, perhaps, the people who live there.

Erecting a proper blind is also a critical matter. An unarmed photographer is foolish to use the same cloth-covered portable blind for grizzlies that he might for deer. A grizzly blind should be in a tree or in some bear-proof cage at ground level. I have used the portable ladder blinds favored by whitetail hunters. Sometimes a motor vehicle might serve as a safe, portable blind.

EQUIPMENT

Bear photography, which is really bear-watching while recording bear behavior, requires a certain amount of basic photo equipment and a knowledge of techniques. In my book *Erwin Bauer's Deer in Their World*, I discuss deer and wildlife photography in great detail, covering everything from film to how to carry equipment in the field. In this chapter, I will discuss photography only as it applies to bears.

The best (if not the only) camera for bear photography is the 35mm single lens reflex, or 35SLR. They are sturdy and fast to operate, neither too heavy nor too bulky, and they are designed to withstand fairly rough handling and abuse in bear country. My own 35SLRs have withstood abnormal heat and sub-zero cold. From long use, the 35SLR bodies feel almost as a part of my hand; using them, as opposed to other, larger cameras, has become second nature.

There are so many efficient, virtually foolproof 35SLRs on the market, with new ones being introduced all the time, that it is impossible to say which manufacturer is best. Today, a beginner can produce bear photos of a quality that eluded veteran wildlife photographers only a generation ago.

For best results, a camera body should have an accurate exposure meter incorporated, with all exposure information visible on the miniature display inside the viewfinder. Usually there is little time for hesitation or fumbling with small details when filming bears. The target is always moving. In fact, many photographers prefer fully automatic 35SLRs (in which the proper exposure is set electronically) when concentrating on bears.

All of the 35SLRs Peggy and I use are of the same model and therefore interchangeable with all of the lenses we carry. Our aim is the greatest possible flexibility and speed in shooting. All of our camera bodies are also equipped with motor drives, which have both advantages and disadvantages. But the disadvantages are relatively minor.

One disadvantage of motor drives is the added weight of the mechanism plus batteries. Another is that, on a few occasions, the mechanical noise has frightened some bears, at least the first or second time they heard it. The big advantage of a motor drive is that it makes tracking a moving animal much easier. It allows the photographer to concentrate on what he sees in his viewfinder.

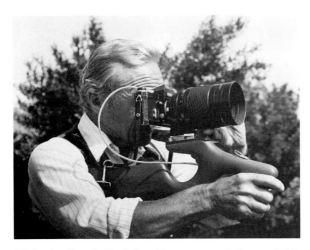

Biologist Frank Craighead has successfully used this gunstock-mounted 35SLR to photograph grizzly behavior in Yellowstone Park.

Leonard Lee Rue III here has a zoom lens mounted on a Monoball tripod attachment.

This is a particularly good camera rig for bear photography, built by Conrad Rowe of Great Falls, Montana. It consists of a gunstock mount (to fit his physique), an attached monopod, and a motor-driven 35SLR with a 300mm f/2.8 telephoto lens. Rowe finds this setup very fast and easy to operate.

ing them difficult to carry along with other gear. And, both must be used with a heavy tripod, monopod, or some other firm base.

The reflex or mirror telephoto is an alternative to the conventional telephoto. These are half as long and weigh only a fraction as much as normal telephoto lenses of the same magnification. They also cost only 10 to 20 percent as much.

Mirror lenses briefly became very popular in the 1970s because of their small size and easy handling. But they were not quite as sharp as other telephotos, and the reflected light in a scene often showed up in small distracting circles in the background of a photo. The mirror lenses were also slow, with a fixed f/stop. Since then, smaller, lighter, and faster reflex telephotos have appeared on the market. One new 500mm mirror lens is not much bigger than my normal 50mm lens. Although the reflexes still don't yet compare in either sharpness or resolution with our favorite telephotos, they still give excellent results. For filming bears, where light weight and fast handling is important, these new mirror lenses are well worth considering—especially by the camera hunter who goes afield for the sport rather than professionally.

Several skilled photographers I know mount their 35SLRs on rifle stocks or similar shoulder-mounted devices when shooting bears. Grizzly biologist Frank Craighead uses a homemade stock cut to fit his own physique. Conrad Rowe of Great Falls, Montana, has designed a handy stock-monopod combination, which is both light and flexible, and on which he can mount any of the several telephoto lenses he owns. Most of these gunstock mounts, which are "fired" by pulling a trigger while focusing with the opposite hand, give excellent results, especially with moving bears. They are far more maneuverable than a heavy tripod. But not all photographers (especially old, hard-headed ones such as the writer) are ever able to really get used to them.

A monopod can be worth its weight in high quality pictures. Look for a lightweight, tubular model that collapses from about 60 inches extended down to 20 inches, so that it can be carried in the hand or in a backpack. Good ones are not expensive. I've used my own monopod as a walking staff over rough terrain and as a wading staff to cross icy creeks. I've often wondered if a monopod couldn't also be designed as a James Bond-style emergency device to frighten away a bear in a too-close encounter.

But for serious bear photography, there is no substitute for a sturdy tripod when filming at very long range, which is most often the case. There isn't yet a preferred outdoor tripod, as there is a preferred outdoor camera, the 35SLR. Nearly all have been designed for studio photography, and they are cumbersome to set up. Until the introduction of the Monoball, most of the tripod heads have been inadequate.

Before buying any tripod, be certain it is absolutely sturdy enough to hold your camera and telephoto lens perfectly steady. Be sure also that your tripod can be set up to stand securely on a steep or uneven slope. The tripod head should hold camera and lens exactly where you point it. It should also allow you to follow the action up or down, right or left, so smoothly that you can concentrate entirely on focus and composition.

Throughout this book I have described the unpredictability of bears, most of which seem to be always in motion. Very few of them are easy or cooperative camera subjects. Getting good pictures depends greatly on skilful, quick camera handling, no matter what kind of equipment you're using. Since skill and speed come only with practice, do plenty of it whenever possible before you ever try to find a bear.

PRACTICE AND PHYSICAL CONDITIONING

It's good advice to go to the local zoo, a game park, or even a baseball or football game, and practice shooting from long range with a telephoto lens. Get the feel of tracking some active target such as a halfback or a dog fetching sticks far away. Shoot empty at first, then progress to black and white film to check your progress. Concentrate on sharp focus as you track a subject. The time you spend beforehand will make a big difference when you eventually have a bear in your viewfinder.

Photo next page: A camera must be fast—and the photographer alert—to catch a grizzly splashing in a cold stream.

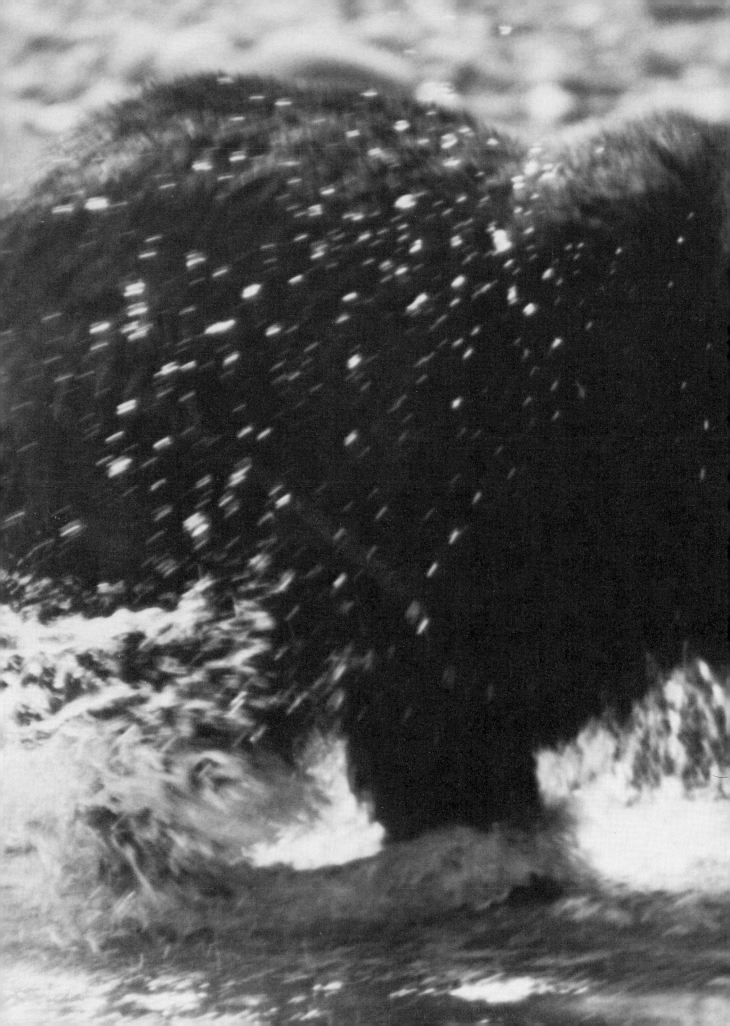

Unlike some other more accommodating creatures, bruins are not always where they are easiest to watch and photograph. You may have to make plenty of footprints on backcountry trails before you spot the first target on a distant hillside. You may also spend hours peering through binoculars. Thus, good physical conditioning, proper footgear, and some kind of camera carrier are as important as the actual photographic equipment. Peggy and I owe many of the photographs in this volume to the fact that we are inveterate hikers and good climbers. We keep in good shape, which is only good sense if you plan to seek a bear.

TRANSPORTATION AND OUTDOOR GEAR

Lately, we have wandered and filmed through bear country in a Volkswagen camper. It is like a hunting camp on wheels, because we can live near anywhere we film. We carry everything we are ever likely to need, from groceries to spare film, sleeping bags and even a small reference library.

Footwear is critical for an itinerant bear hunter. The shoes we depend on most are sturdy ankle-high hiking boots with lug-type soles. The leather is so well broken-in it feels as if it's part of the foot. For colder, wet or snowy weather, we also have insulated and waterproof boots. We always carry two pairs of rubber hipboots as well. Peggy and I could not possibly have walked within range of the McNeil River brown bears seen in Chapter 3 without hipboots or waders.

The carrier I prefer is a light, external-frame backpack with many separate compartments. Those compartments keep exposed film apart from unexposed, extra lenses apart from high calorie snacks, and insect repellent apart from a canteen of water. The backpack also contains an ultra-light rainsuit, sunglasses, gloves, and matches in a waterproof container. If we do not plan to travel as far on foot, or stay as long, we use beltpacks instead of backpacks.

AVOIDING SURPRISES

Only a fool would walk blindly through bear country, particularly grizzly or brown-bear country. The odds against any trouble are staggering,

Good rugged binoculars such as the rubber-armored, waterproof Clear View 8×40s or 10×40s let a photographer scan a distant landscape to locate a target. The waterproof feature is doubly important in damp, grizzly-bear country.

but there is still the remote possibility. The worst thing is that the unobservant hiker or photographer might miss viewing the bears or other creatures on the scene. Peggy and I hike briskly, but we also stop at regular intervals to study the landscape. That is good advice to anyone, particularly when in areas known to contain grizzlies. From long experience, I also advise strictly observing the following rules.

When in bear country, stay in the open as much as possible, so that you have the widest unobstructed vision all around. Be doubly alert when traveling into the wind, especially into a strong or rushing wind, when a bear may not get your scent and be unaware of your approach. Never surprise a bear. Avoid known or obvious food sources such as berry patches and animal carcasses. Watch also for fresh bear sign, such as tracks, diggings and scats, or droppings.

If you detect the foul odor of decomposing meat while on the trail, stop. It's a cinch that a

Loaded for the bear, the photographer is equipped to shoot a variety of bonus animals, such as this red fox, devouring a ground squirrel.

Leonard Lee Rue III here models the ideal wildlife-photographer's vest he designed and now markets from his home in Blairstown, New Jersey. The vest's 19 pockets will hold extra lenses, many rolls of film, lunch and raingear.

The Rue vest, also shown above, features a ventilated back and Velcro-fastened back cover for inclement weather, shown here being inserted into a back pocket.

bear has already smelled it, and is probably on the carcass, be it moose, caribou, sheep, or whatever. Try to avoid the area entirely, if possible. Brown and grizzly bears can be particularly short-tempered where food is concerned. If you approach a food cache from upwind and don't smell it, you're sure to recognize it when you see it. Bears often cover their food with branches and forest litter and bed nearby until they've eaten all of it. If you stumble onto such a semi-concealed cache, leave as quietly and quickly as possible.

CUBS

If there is one thing you should avoid it is approaching a cub, even a cub that comes curiously toward you. Mother bears of threatened cubs are the most terrible creatures to meet on a North American trail. Give them a wide berth and then some. It is true that attacks by female bears tend to result in disfigurement rather than death, but that is small consolation.

DOGS

Although dogs have on occasion helped save people from bears, as a rule you should never take a dog, even a courageous one, into bear backcountry. Some black bears may run from a dog, but more often the sight and smell of a dog will only infuriate a grizzly and may bring on an attack. No dog is a match for an angry grizzly or brown bear. When in trouble, a pet's first instinct is to come running back directly to its master. In British Columbia, a female grizzly killed a Brittany spaniel at the base of a tree in which its owner, an amateur nature photographer, had taken refuge when his dog came running for protection. Anyway, free-running dogs aren't allowed on most park and refuge trails.

FOOD AND BLOOD ODORS

We have camped for many hundreds of nights in bear country. On several occasions, the ani-

While I was looking for bear on the American River in Alaska, this pale wolf suddenly emerged .

This heavy metal, bear-proof communal food cache has been installed at Teklanika Campground, Denali National Park, Alaska. Campers can store their edibles here—free—safely away from tents and campsites. The cache is a good idea that would be practical in any bear country.

mals have prowled just beyond the canvas at night. But we have never been molested, and we like to believe it is because we invariably keep an absolutely clean camp, free of food and food odor. We do not cook in our tent. We hang food out of reach, far from the actual sleeping place, or we lock it securely in our car. In a tent camp, we do not sleep in the same clothing we wore when cooking.

The plain fact is that more bear incidents across the continent take place around heavily-used campgrounds than anywhere else. Even though we may keep a clean campsite, we have no way of controlling the sanitation of those who have used the same spot before us or are camping close by. The only thing to do is to be extraordinarily careful and select a campsite only after checking it out for garbage and sign of bears.

After an uneventful morning in a photo blind, we found a black bear trying to enter our VW camper parked not far away. The repair bill for the window trim and grill was modest.

Stay far from obviously slovenly campers. Never pitch your own tent near bear sign, new or old, and avoid the vicinity of bear trails and garbage receptacles. More and more nowadays, national park authorities in both Canadian and U.S. national parks are installing garbage devices that are virtually bearproof. In Denali National Park, there are also locking compartmented food caches made of heavy-gauge metal available free for campers at Teklanika Campground, which is in the center of prime grizzly range.

When in bear country, depend on less odorous foods such as those of the freeze-dried variety. Also, everything packed into any campground should be packed out. Burying wastes is as dangerous as it is useless. A bear can easily smell these things and dig up the offal. And that same bear can become a menace to the next group of campers who pitch a tent on or near that spot.

There is an old Indian saying that whenever a leaf falls in the forest, the hawk sees it, the deer hears it, and the bear smells it. Bears do have an incredibly good sense of smell that leads them to even the faintest promise of food.

There is some indication that odors other than cooking aromas attract bears. Perfumes, deoderants, and other sweet-smelling lotions may very well intrigue bears, so it seems foolish to wear them in bear country. Keep sleeping bags free of those same unnatural cosmetic odors. On the other hand, human body odors from sweat may have an opposite, repelling effect. The smell of human urine may also repel bruins. Some bear researchers strongly believe that women should stay out of bear country during their menstrual periods, and that human sexual activity in a camp may attract bears; others regard this as pure bunk.

HUMAN NOISE

Park officials almost everywhere urge visitors in bear country to travel in a group and carry along noisemakers such as bells or tin cans containing loose pebbles. The first is good advice, but I'm not so certain about the second.

We know of very few times when a bear ever attacked a group of people. A bear may be intimidated by the larger mass. Noise may alert some bruins that a human is approaching, and give the animal time to move away with dignity. But that is only a thin theory. The same bell or tinkling sound can also tell a bear that a sackful of chocolate and granola is coming down the trail. When Peggy and I find it necessary to pass through a dense cover in grizzly country, we shout just in case that is helpful. I wish I knew if it ever was.

COPING WITH AGGRESSIVE BEARS

There is no guaranteed lifesaving method for coping with an aggressive bear. But some tactics have proven more successful than others. Keep in mind that a bruin rearing on its hind legs is not always aggressive. If it moves its head from side to side, or slowly up and down, it may only be trying to get a better scent or to focus on you with nearsighted eyes. Usually the best response is to remain still and to speak in soft, even tones. The bear might get the idea that you mean no harm and are not a threat. It might even bluff a

charge, but at the last minute veer away and leave the scene.

Look around and think about your surroundings. When a bear suddenly looms near, look for trees before you act. Of course it's not easy to remain calm in such a spot, but stonewall as long as you are able, keeping in mind that black bears can also climb. Do not try to run. Remember, any healthy adult bear can run faster over rough ground than a racehorse on a track. Running may also stimulate the bear to give chase, which it might not do otherwise.

If you are carrying a pack or camera equipment when you suddenly face a threatening bear, there is another tactic that has often worked. Remove the pack slowly and deliberately, and set it on the ground as you slowly back away. That can distract the animal long enough for you to reach a tree and climb up into it.

Not removing a pack has also prevented serious injury and even saved a number of lives. When there is no other escape and a bear is almost upon you, your last resort is to play dead. Drop to the ground face-down. Lift your knees up to cover your chest and stomach, and clasp your hands around the back of your neck. Wearing your pack will shield much of your torso. Often bears have inflicted only minor injuries on humans crouched unresisting in this position. The main goal should be to keep the bear's claws away from your head and neck.

I have had a number of encounters with bears, browns usually, which never threatened my life but still left me liquid in the knees. Almost all of these occurred near streams where I suddenly came upon the animal, or vice versa. That was often because the riverine brush was heavy, and because the noisy rush of the water muffled all other noise. The older and wiser I've grown, the more cautious I've become in bear country when the noise of wind or water is loud.

FIREARMS

Then there is the matter of hikers and photographers carrying firearms when in grizzly country. Firearms are correctly forbidden in national parks, which settles the matter in these sanctuaries. But are they good policy elsewhere? There are good arguments pro and con.

An adequate firearm would be a comfort in the hands of someone who is also an experienced shooter. But there is also the possibility that a magnum pistol on the hip would encourage the carrier to behave less wisely with a bear than if unarmed. I'll admit there have been a few times when I would have felt vastly better with a gun in my pack when alone on a wilderness mountainside. But Peggy and I have opted never to carry arms; by using common sense in the presence of bears, we have never needed one.

Andy Russell, an old-time author, hunting guide, and motion-picture bear photographer of southern Alberta, always believed that bears could somehow tell whether or not he was carrying a gun. He once wrote: "The mere fact of having a gun within reach, even cached somewhere in a pack or hidden holster, causes a man to act with unconscious arrogance, and thus maybe to smell different, or to transmit some kind of signal objectionable to bears." Strange as it may seem, there is a consensus among those who have thoroughly studied grizzlies that the animals certainly might be able to detect a person's intentions and maybe even his fears. I suspect that an unarmed photographer has better odds of shooting good bear pictures than a photographer carrying a gun.

BEAR DETERRENTS

Sometime in the future, people who venture nervously into bear country may be able to carry extra "courage." Researchers are working on a number of new products designed to deter bears encountered in the wilderness.

We know photographers who carry their own bear deterrents. One photographer always has a container of mace handy in his backpack. Another cameraman carries an aerosol foghorn, which is one of the emergency signaling devices carried aboard small boats. But neither of these men knows if the mace or the sudden deafening noise will really drive a determined grizzly away. They haven't had to use them.

Dr. Charles Jonkel of Montana University's Border Grizzly Project has been testing bear repellents and deterrents for ten years. Dr. Fred Dean at the University of Alaska has long been interested in the same goal. So far, neither has come up with a product guaranteed to work. But both caution against relying on the bear-repelling concoctions now on the market, although the scientists admit these might possibly be worthwhile.

One such product, composed mostly of concentrated red pepper compressed in a container resembling a fire extinguisher, may have saved one biologist from a serious grizzly mauling in Yellowstone Park. According to Richard Knight, head of the Interagency Grizzly Bear Team, the man was working in Hayden Valley when he was charged by a grizzly he had been watching. He sprayed the bruin in close range with the red-pepper solution, and although the bruin knocked him down and bit him on the leg, it turned away and left the area. Knight is not at all positive that the bear retreated because of the spray. Nevertheless, he ordered more of the pepper canisters for other grizzly researchers.

Martin Smith, an undergraduate student on Jonkel's project, believes that the red-pepper chemical (called Animal Repel and developed by Tony Musso in Florida) seems to be the most effective bear deterrent tested so far. He has also tested boat horns, ammonia spray, tear gas, and rubber bullets fired from tear-gas guns, but he is not yet ready to comment publicly on any of these.

One starry night, Roy Olander was camped in California's High Sierra, but he couldn't truly enjoy it. Black bears had rampaged through another campsite nearby and he tossed about, wondering if they would soon bother him. He also wondered if something couldn't be devised to keep bears away and make camping more care-free. After five years of sticky, stinky tinkering in his garage, the high school science teacher believes he has at last discovered a biologically and ecologically sound way for outdoor enthusiasts to keep bears at a safe distance. Olander calls his synthetic skunk "juice" Bear Skunker, and he claims bears find it totally unbearable.

Olander started his studies with dead skunks turned over to him by friendly animal control officers. In deference to his neighbors, he worked in a sealed glass experiment capsule with an air scrubber attached. His aim was to duplicate and perhaps even fortify real skunk stench. So far,

Peggy and I erected this hasty cloth blind to photograph a ruffed grouse drumming on a log. Unaccountably, a black bear ripped it apart one night.

says Olander, Bear Skunker has worked perfectly on the six bears tested. Olander has been unable to market the product, however, because Environmental Protection Agency officials want more evidence of the spray's effectiveness and also want to test it for toxicity. EPA biologist Daniel Peacock (no relationship to grizzly man Doug) said he is concerned about the safety of one of the ingredients in Bear Skunker.

A firm in Montana called the Mountain Scent and Bugle Manufacturing Company has developed a device to fence problem bears away from livestock. In some later modified form, it might also keep bears away from campers and other people overnighting in bear country. But right now, owner Loren Butler does not recommend it for campsite use.

The device is mainly a ½-inch-wide metal band connected to a 2-pound storage battery. It is used in combination with a bait called 10-Dead Horse, which is saturated onto cotton swabs stuck into the metal bands. A bear is thus enticed to touch or lick the band with tongue or wet nose

and ... *zowie* ... 5,000 volts at low amperage jolt the animal. According to Butler, 14 different grizzlies have investigated the device, and not one has ever come back. But the trouble is that a grizzly goes completely berserk for a few moments after the lightning strikes, attacking everything within the immediate area before it clears out.

"If you were nearby when it happened," Butler says, smiling, "you would damn well want to be watching from the top of a very tall tree."

Someday, battery-powered stun guns similar to those that police use to subdue people may prove effective as bear-attack deterrents. The charge released from these guns disrupts the victim's central nervous system.

A WORD TO THE WISE

Coping with bears and especially photographing them is an uncertain, sometimes uneasy, but terribly fascinating business. More than anything else, it requires caution and common sense.

BIBLIOGRAPHY

Bears—Their Biology and Management (Papers of the Fourth International Conference on Bear Research and Management). Kalispell, Montana: 1977.

Craighead, Frank C., Jr. *Track of the Grizzly*. San Francisco: Sierra Club Books, 1979.

Cramond, Mike. *Killer Bears*. New York: Outdoor Life Books, Times Mirror Magazines Inc., 1981.

Dalrymple, Byron, with photos by Erwin A. Bauer. *North American Big Game Animals*. New York: Outdoor Life Books, Times Mirror Magazines, Inc., 1985.

Davids, Richard C., with photography by Dan Guravich. *Lords of the Arctic*. New York: Macmillan Publishing Co., Inc., 1982.

Dufresne, Frank, with drawings by Rachel S. Horne. *No Room for Bears*. New York: Holt, Rinehart and Winston, 1965.

Kaniut, Larry. *Alaska Bear Tales*. Anchorage: Alaska Northwest Publishing Co., 1983.

Larsen, Thor. *The World of the Polar Bear*. London: The Hanlyn Publishing Group, Ltd., 1978.

Laycock, George, illustrated by Nancy Grossman. *Big Nick*. New York: W.W. Norton & Co., 1967.

McCracken, Harold. *The Beast That Walks Like a Man*. Garden City, New York: Hanover House, 1955.

Nesbitt, Wm. H., and Philip L. Wright, eds. *Records of North American Big Game*, eighth edition. Alexandria, Virginia: The Boone and Crockett Club, 1981.

Ormond, Clyde. *Bear!* Harrisburg: The Stackpole Co., 1961.

Perry, Richard. *Bears: The World of Animals*. London: Arthur Barker, Ltd., and New York City: Arco Publishing Co., 1970.

Rue, Leonard Lee III. *How I Photograph Wildlife and Nature*. New York and London: W.W. Norton & Co., 1984.

Schneider, Bill. *Where the Grizzly Walks*. Missoula: Mountain Press Publishing Co., 1977.

Shaw, John. *The Nature Photographer's Complete Guide to Professional Field Techniques*. New York: Amphoto, Watson-Guptill Publications, 1984.

Wright, William H. *The Grizzly Bear*. New York: Charles Scribner's Sons, 1909.

Young, F.M. *Man Meets Grizzly*. Boston: Houghton Mifflin Co., 1980.

EQUIPMENT SOURCES

Based on extensive field testing, the author can recommend the following sources of outdoor and photo gear. Most offer catalogs and sell by mail-order.

General gear:

Burnham Brothers, PO Box 669, Marble Falls, TX 76854

Camp Trails Packs, Box 966, Binghamton, NY 13902

Coleman Company, 250 North St. Francis, Wichita, KS 67201

Early Winters, 110 Prefontaine Place South, Seattle, WA 98104

R.E.I., PO Box 88125, Seattle, WA 98188

Photo blinds:

Baker Tree Stands, PO Box 1003, Valdosta, GA 31601

EUREKA! Tents, PO Box 966, Binghamton, NY 13902

Leonard Rue Enterprises, RD 3, Box 31, Blairstown, NJ 07825. (Offers wildlife photo accessories, including Rue-designed camera gunstock, camouflaged vests and blinds, deer scents, more.)

Camera lenses:

Clear View Sports & Optics, PO Box 279, Hazel Park, MI 48030

Vivitar Corp., PO Box 2100, Santa Monica, CA 90406

INDEX